THE

NORDSTROM WAY

THE

NORDSTROM WAY

TO CUSTOMER EXPERIENCE EXCELLENCE

THIRD EDITION

CREATING A VALUES-DRIVEN SERVICE CULTURE

ROBERT SPECTOR & BREANNE O. REEVES

WILEY

Published by John Wiley & Sons, Inc., Hoboken, New Jersey.
Published simultaneously in Canada

For general information about our other products and services, please contact our Customer Care Department within the United States at (800) 762-2974, outside the United States at (317) 572-3993 or fax (317) 572-4002.

Wiley publishes in a variety of print and electronic formats and by print-on-demand. Some material included with standard print versions of this book may not be included in e-books or in print-on-demand. If this book refers to media such as a CD or DVD that is not included in the version you purchased, you may download this material at http://booksupport.wiley.com. For more information about Wiley products, visit www.wiley.com.

Library of Congress Cataloging-in-Publication Data:

Names: Spector, Robert, 1947– author. | Reeves, breAnne O., 1980– author.
Title: Nordstrom way to customer experience excellence : creating a
  values-driven service culture / Robert Spector, breAnne O. Reeves.
Other titles: Nordstrom way to customer service excellence
Description: Third edition. | Hoboken, New Jersey : John Wiley & Sons, Inc.,
  [2017] | Earlier edition published as: The Nordstrom way to customer
  service excellence : a handbook for implementing great service in your
  organization. | Includes bibliographical references and index. |
  Identifiers: LCCN 2017019609 (print) | LCCN 2017033173 (ebook) | ISBN
  9781119375371 (pdf) | ISBN 9781119375388 (epub) | ISBN 9781119375357 (pbk.)
Subjects: LCSH: Customer services—United States—Handbooks, manuals, etc. |
  Nordstrom (Firm)—Management. | Department stores—United
  States—Management.
Classification: LCC HF5415.5 (ebook) | LCC HF5415.5 .S626785 2017 (print) |
  DDC 658.8/12—dc23
LC record available at https://lccn.loc.gov/2017019609

Cover Design: RSi

Printed in the United States of America

C10011963_070919

In loving memory of my parents,
Fred and Florence Spector,
who taught me The Spector Way:
Work hard, be good, do well.
—R.S.

Thank you, Clara June Reynolds,
for reminding me every single day,
to stay silly, be nice, put others first,
enjoy life, and most importantly, have fun!
—B.O.R.

"Your beliefs become your thoughts,
Your thoughts become your words,
Your words become your actions,
Your actions become your habits,
Your habits become your values,
Your values become your destiny."

—Mahatma Gandhi

Contents

Acknowledgments

My Nordstrom journey began in 1982, when I became the regular freelance correspondent in Seattle for *Women's Wear Daily* and the other trade newspapers that then comprised Fairchild Publications.

One of the first companies I wrote about was Nordstrom, which was then a strictly West Coast retail chain, but was beginning to gain a national reputation for its culture of customer service. As a native of New Jersey, whose first job out of college was writing retail advertising for Bamberger's department store (a division of Macy's), I was fascinated by the Nordstrom culture of taking care of the customer. I remain fascinated to this day.

In 1990, I was contacted by Elizabeth Wales, a Seattle literary agent, whose next-door neighbor was Patrick McCarthy, then Nordstrom's number one salesperson. Elizabeth asked me if I'd be interested in writing the book with Patrick. You know what my answer was. Five years later, John Wiley & Sons published *The Nordstrom Way: The Inside Story of America's Number One Customer Service Company*. It quickly became a bestseller, and it changed the course of my life.

As a keynote speaker, I've had an opportunity to speak to every kind of business you can imagine (and some you can't imagine) throughout the United States as well as in 26 countries. It's been quite a ride!

And as an author, I've had the unique opportunity to periodically revisit Nordstrom, both literally and figuratively (as we explain in greater detail in the Introduction). Each time I research and write a version of *The Nordstrom Way*, I learn something new. Each time I learn something new, I have something new to teach. Over the past few years, I have shifted some of my time to teaching business students at the University of Washington's Bothell campus, and at Western Washington University in Bellingham. I believe that it's essential for students to not only understand traditional business skills but also to understand what it means to operate a business or to be a stellar employee—viewed through the lens of these values that we have identified that are crucial to Nordstrom's success. I tell my students that regardless of whatever field they choose, the values of The Nordstrom Way will serve them well.

I've also had the opportunity to be an adviser and thought leader to organizations large and small around the world. I particularly enjoy the breakout ideation sessions where people at every level of the organization are given the opportunity to brainstorm on how they can help their organization become the Nordstrom of their industry. After leading and observing these brainstorming sessions, where people talk about how they can do their jobs better, I've come away with what I call the Three Immutable Truths:

1. Most people want to do a good job.
2. Most people want to be a part of something bigger than themselves.
3. It's up to management to make sure that people feel valued and appreciated so that they come to work every day with a desire to do a good job and to be a part of something bigger than themselves.

With all of that as a backdrop, I want to acknowledge all the people who helped to make possible all the versions of *The Nordstrom Way*. Deep and heartfelt thanks to:

Patrick McCarthy for his belief in The Nordstrom Way and for his shining example for generations of Nordstrom employees.
The cochairmen of the third generation—Bruce, John N., Jim, and Jack McMillan—for their cooperation and trust in the original book and for the use of three privately published family memoirs.

Acknowledgments

The leadership of the fourth generation—Blake, Pete, Erik, and Jamie—
for continuing that cooperation and trust and for sharing their
insights.

Special thanks to Brooke White, who selflessly ran Nordstrom's public
relations department for many years, and who was an invaluable
ally in helping me get what I needed in order to tell the Nordstrom
story in the most accurate and up-to-date way. She never demurred
at my inevitable "one more thing" requests. Without Brooke, these
books would be incomplete.

Kellie Tormey, Brooke's predecessor, who was there for the original
book and was also a great supporter and helper.

All the other people in Nordstrom's public relations department who
helped us with requests over the years. Special thanks for this edition
goes to Brenna Sussman.

David Marriott for his assistance in helping get this project off the
ground.

Richard Narramore, our editor, for shepherding this project with the
highest professionalism and for giving us the rare opportunity to
revisit, reshape, revise, and expand this material—on more than one
occasion.

Elizabeth Wales, a stalwart and supportive agent and friend, who has
been there every step of the way.

Marybeth Spector, my wife and my friend, who has lived through every
incarnation of *The Nordstrom Way*.

And breAnne O. Reeves, my business partner, cofounder of our company RSi, and coauthor, for helping to make me a better person
and for making me laugh.

ROBERT SPECTOR
Bellingham, Washington

My Nordstrom adventure began in 2009, when I met Robert Spector. After a successful run in the corporate sales and marketing world, I decided to venture out and start my own business(es). I swore that I would *never* sit through another sales training, keynote, or "sales rally" again. I swore I would never sell anything to anyone that they did not need.

After a fateful meeting with Robert and after many happy-hour conversations over glasses of wine, Robert hired my modest firm to support the launch of his newest book, *The Mom & Pop Store*. We were tasked with hosting the book's first launch party, to be held at Capers, a home-furnishings store in West Seattle, where we were both living at the time. Most book launch events go a little like this: show up, schmooze with the author, get a book signed, have a paper cup full of coffee, tea, or wine, then leave.

Well, I had a different idea of what a book signing should look like. Maybe this is the Nordstrom in my blood. My team and I took it upon ourselves to get to know Robert and find out where he got his morning coffee, his afternoon sandwich, his happy hour, and oh so much more. How's that for getting to know a client?

We continued on our Nordstrom Way journey by having each of his favorite mom-and-pop establishments run a special the day of his book launch in West Seattle: His fave coffee beverage at Hotwire Coffee, his fave breakfast plate at Easy Street, his fave sandwich at Husky Deli, his fave cocktail at Fresh Bistro. You get the point. Additionally, we had Elliot Bay Brewing provide a keg of his fave Northwest beer, and Northwest wine as well. We packed the house. Everyone had a great time. And guess what? It had nothing to do with the book. Or Robert. It had to do with the customer experience. It had to do with partners and vendors. It had everything to do with caring about others.

Aha moment number one: I need to read *The Nordstrom Way*.

Acknowledgments

Aha moment number two: The Nordstrom Way is more than a book. It is more than a keynote. Let's create platforms to help companies around the world become better based on this knowledge.

During one of our many meetings, Robert asked me a life-changing question: "Would you like to own half of *The Nordstrom Way*?" I said, uh, *yes*! The thought of leveraging the material from *The Nordstrom Way* in order to support the success of others was beyond provocative to me. From then on, my focus was on digging into the culture of Nordstrom and sorting out the values that make Nordstrom what it is.

As we identified the values that sustainably drive Nordstrom, I could not help but compare them to my family and upbringing. This was the moment when I knew for sure that I was in the right business.

Empower people to be good and do good. It is that simple.

I would like to thank:

The Nordstrom team that helped to make this happen.

Richard Narramore, our editor, for putting up with our persistence regarding design and marketing, amongst many other things.

My humble and amazing parents, Mark and Melodye Reeves. When people ask the question: "Who trains Nordstrom employees?" Nordstrom answers, "their parents." My parents taught me "the way."

Robert Spector, my business partner, and coauthor, for inviting me to participate in this project.

And, my husband and best friend, Silas Reynolds, who inspires me to be the best human on the planet every single day.

BREANNE O. REEVES
Bellingham, Washington

Foreword

As a Seattle native, I've had a front-row seat to Nordstrom's growth from our little corner of the world to 39 states, three Canadian provinces, and one commonwealth, while earning an international reputation (with online customers in almost 100 countries!) for providing the gold standard in customer service experience.

I've had the pleasure of knowing several members of the Nordstrom family and I've expressed to them my admiration for how they conduct their business. Nordstrom, like Starbucks, exemplifies our Northwest values that combine competitiveness with caring.

In our hypercompetitive, ever-changing, ever-challenging retail world, where concepts come and go and where competitors rise and fall, how has Nordstrom been able to survive and thrive for almost 120 years? Robert Spector and breAnne O. Reeves provide the simple answers to this existential question.

As the subtitle indicates, this is a book about creating a values-driven, service-obsessed corporate culture that encourages, motivates, rewards, recognizes, and compensates employees to consistently deliver a world-class experience to customers, one customer at a time.

As the world economy becomes more and more about relationships and connections that are built on the foundation of trust and respect, Nordstrom's principles of personal leadership are more important and relevant than ever.

At Starbucks, we believe what Nordstrom believes: *The employee experience determines the customer experience.* If you regard employees and customers as human beings, everything else will take care of itself. It's an article of faith that if you engage your staff as partners (not assets or labor costs), they will achieve results beyond what is thought possible.

Through four generations of family leadership, the Nordstroms have shown that they know who they are, and that they know the kind of people they want to attract to their team. The Nordstroms bring clarity and honesty in regard to who they are, where they want to go, and how they're going to get there. They are clear about their purpose, values, and goals, and they draw people who are aligned (both individually and collectively) with the very same purpose, values, and goals.

Culture is a funny thing. Changing it is not about talking about it; it's about living it. People will rise or fall to the expectations that the organizational culture puts on them. If cultural expectations are high, the chances are good that they will be met. Conversely, if expectations are low, those expectations will also be met.

Nordstrom believes in doing the right thing. The company seeks out people who want to do all the right things for all the right reasons. They seek out individuals who can think independently and who make the goal of creating a satisfied customer their highest priority. Nordstrom believes in throwing out the rules—real and imagined—and promoting empowerment and autonomous thinking. This philosophy is epitomized in their only rule: "Use Good Judgment in All Situations."

In many cases, in most organizations, the rulebook goes way too far. It tries to tell people how to be instead of explaining what they're trying to do. At Starbucks, we always said that we need "recipes, not rules."

Again, clarity of purpose is essential. Nordstrom is clear that every decision the company makes is for the benefit of customers, and that Nordstrom employees—both on the frontlines and in support—are crucial to enhancing the customer experience.

Trust is the cornerstone of all human interaction, be it social, emotional, or commercial. Caring—for coworkers and customers—is a sign of strength. Without trust and caring we'll never know what could have been possible in our organization.

High-trust companies hold their people accountable, treat them like responsible adults, and encourage them to take ownership of the customer experience. They want their people to be true to themselves and to their values. Positive actions and decisions build trust and show that you care. The best Nordstrom sales associates will do virtually everything he or she can to make sure a shopper leaves the store a satisfied customer. As my friend Bruce Nordstrom says, "The happiest customer is the one who leaves the store carrying a Nordstrom shopping bag."

"Servant Leadership" is a philosophy and set of practices that I have tried to adhere to—from the days of watching my parents running their small grocery store in Seattle, to all my years at Starbucks, to the life I live today as an author, speaker, and mentor. The Nordstrom family and every successful Nordstrom manager, buyer, and executive represent the ideal of servant leadership. We are here to serve and support our team, not the other way around.

At Starbucks, we believe that there is no conflict between treating your people with respect and dignity and making a profit. We simply stated that respect and dignity are essential, which is why respect and dignity were factored into the price of every cup of coffee we sold.

Robert and breAnne have identified core cultural values that are absolute necessities for every organization: trust, respect, loyalty, awareness, humility, communication and collaboration, competition and compensation, innovation and adaptation, and give back and have fun. We can all agree that these values are essential to loyalty and longevity.

In this compelling and entertaining book, Robert Spector and breAnne O. Reeves show how any organization—including yours—can create a lasting customer service culture by attracting people who buy into your nonnegotiable core values.

Chock-full of stories of exemplary customer service, unselfish teamwork, fearless innovation, community and global citizenship, and good old-fashioned fun, this book will make you laugh, shed a tear or two, and convince you that your organization has the potential to become the "Nordstrom" of your industry.

If that's your goal, what better time to start than right now?

HOWARD BEHAR, retired president,
Starbucks North America and Starbucks International

Introduction

A few years ago, Blake Nordstrom, copresident of the company with his two brothers, scheduled a lunch with the chief executive officer of another famous Seattle company. The CEO asked Blake if he wouldn't mind stopping by the tailor shop of the downtown Seattle Nordstrom flagship store on his way to the lunch, and bring with him a couple of pairs of slacks that the CEO had arranged to have altered.

"Blake said, 'Sure, no problem,'" the CEO remembered. By the time the two executives met for lunch, both of them had forgotten about the pants. "That evening at nine o'clock, there's a knock at my door. There's Blake with those two pairs of pants. I said, 'Man, that's what I call service.'"

In a sense, Blake's personally delivering those pants is the perfect metaphor for The Nordstrom Way. Nordstrom's culture encourages entrepreneurial, motivated men and women to make the extra effort to give customer service that is unequaled. "Not service like it used to be, but service that never was," reported Morley Safer in a profile of the company on the CBS television program *60 Minutes*. "A place where service is an act of faith."

Morley Safer made that observation in 1990. Although much has changed since then, Nordstrom's commitment to service has never wavered.

When *The Nordstrom Way* was first published in 1995, it struck a chord with countless organizations in a broad variety of industries all over the world. Many hundreds of thousands of copies and four iterations later, *The Nordstrom Way* continues to serve as an inspiration for virtually every sector of international business. Nordstrom endures as a standard against which other companies and organizations privately (and often publicly) measure themselves.

"If all businesses could be like Nordstrom," said Harry Mullikin, chairman emeritus of Westin Hotels, "it would change the whole economy of this country."

"The Nordstrom Way," the phrase that we have helped to popularize, is shorthand for a customer experience that is *sui generis*. Through all the changes that Nordstrom and the retail industry have gone through over more than a century, the Nordstrom Way is still in a class by itself.

It must be noted that Nordstrom did not suggest we write *The Nordstrom Way* nor did the company commission its publication. Nevertheless, when the original book was written, the company made its top executives, managers, and salespeople available for interviews. Through all the different versions of this book that we have written over the years (which we will explain in greater detail), Nordstrom has cooperated in helping us to tell their ever-evolving story.

Introduction to the Third Edition

This is a completely different book from the first and second editions, just as the first and second editions were completely different from the 1995 book and the 1997 trade paperback.

In 2005, for the 10th anniversary of the original publication, we initially thought of adding a new chapter or two. But upon reviewing the material, it was obvious that much of the book was too dated to be relevant. For example, the original book didn't mention something called the Internet. By 2012, the 2005 first edition was also dated. Hence, the necessity for the book you are now reading. Our books have evolved just as Nordstrom has evolved. Our books reflect both Nordstrom's bedrock culture and its understanding that survival requires perpetual adaptation and evolution.

This third edition is coauthored by breAnne O. Reeves, cofounder and partner of our consulting company RSi, a thought leader in customer experience. This book is her vision, based on our years of research and working with clients in many different business sectors all over the world.

The Customer Experience Conundrum

This is not a book about selling shoes or clothes or cosmetics or jewelry. As the subtitle spells out, this is a book about creating a values-driven, service-obsessed corporate culture that encourages, motivates, rewards, recognizes, and compensates employees to consistently deliver a world-class experience to customers.

Each one of us is an expert on customer service. At one point or another during the course of our day, every one of us plays the role of the customer. We all know the difference between good service and bad service. You don't have to read yet another book to understand this.

So, then, why is good customer service so rare?

Picture in your mind a customer service counter. On one side of the counter is you, the customer. You know exactly what your expectations are: a good product or service at a fair price. If there's a problem, you want it taken care of as quickly, seamlessly, and painlessly as possible. Simple stuff, right?

But a funny thing happens to people when they move to the other side of the customer service counter (or the front desk or the reception area or the phone or Internet) where they are the ones who are giving service as opposed to receiving it. Unfortunately, this is the place where their behaviors are determined and dominated by the rules, the process, the manual, the bureaucracy, the way it's always been done:

"Sorry, that's against our policy."

"Sorry, we have a rule against that."

"Sorry, my manager's off today. Can I get back to you when she gets back?"

When we are customers, we don't want to hear those excuses. So when we are dealing with our customers, why would we want to offer up these lame excuses to our customers? It's as if someone hit the "delete" button on our customer service memory. We forget about the Golden Rule, about empathy, about the customer's experience. Because organizations are so wrapped up in the day-to-day minutiae, it's difficult for them to consistently give customer service.

Although we all know that the key to success is a satisfied customer, few of us are as single-minded as Nordstrom in creating and sustaining a customer-obsessed culture and hiring people who fit the culture and who happily provide that exemplary service—because it's demanded and expected of them.

When it comes to singing the song of customer service, anyone can recite the words but few can carry the tune.

Becoming the Nordstrom of Your Industry

Most companies, large and small, base their business model on their own internal systems. These systems are set up to make life easier for the company not necessarily for the customer.

One three-panel *Dilbert* cartoon strip, by Scott Adams, illustrates this mind-set. In the first panel, the lead employee tells two others: "Our goal is to ship a million units this quarter." In the second panel, another employee asks: "Do we have any goals that involve making customers happy?" In the third panel, the lead employee responds: "I'm talking about *our* goals; not *theirs*."

When we show that cartoon strip in our keynotes and training sessions it inevitably gets a knowing laugh from the audience. It's funny because it's true. Too true.

On the other hand, because Nordstrom is dedicated to making life easier for the customer, it believes its job is to adjust to the customers' needs at the time of the purchasing decision. Nordstrom doesn't determine what good service is; the customer does.

"From the sales floor to support, no matter where we work, our challenge is to constantly put the customer at the center of everything we do," said Blake Nordstrom, who runs the company with his brothers Pete and Erik. "The ultimate filter for all our efforts should be: 'How is this meaningful to the customer and will it increase sales?' If something is important to the customer, we should find a way to deliver it. If it's not important to the customer, we need to question if it's worth our time and focus."

Nordstrom has no official mission statement or value statement, "because sometimes that becomes the flavor of the month," said Blake. Mission statements "are only as good as the words on the paper."

Nordstrom is customer-driven not customer-focused. "Customer-driven" means that Nordstrom puts the needs of the customer in the center of every decision on how and where to allocate resources. It means putting the customer in the driver's seat and setting aside notions and historical preconceptions of how the customer wants to be served. Customer driven is about empowering customers to dictate their terms when it comes to the different ways they choose to shop.

This mind-set is significant because of the astonishing speed with which the shopping experience is changing and how customers are reconsidering the service experience. Customers want to do business with companies that swiftly recognize and respond to their needs and desires.

Nordstrom has been ranked as a retail industry leader in customer satisfaction by the American Customer Satisfaction Survey in each and every year since 1995. Nordstrom has consistently ranked as America's favorite fashion retailer in Market Force Information's annual survey, which cited Nordstrom as the industry pacesetter in (1) service, (2) ease of shopping, (3) ambience, and (4) brand value.

Nordstrom has long been a popular subject for study among authors of customer service books and educators at business graduate schools such as Harvard and Wharton. *Roll Call*, the newspaper of Capitol Hill, once advised press aides for members of the United States Congress to use the "Nordstrom approach" when trying to sell producers of political talk shows on the benefits of booking their bosses. The *New York Times Magazine* noted that a minister in Bel Air, California, told his congregation in a Sunday sermon that Nordstrom, "carries out the call of the gospel in ways more consistent and caring than we sometimes do in the church."

In an article in the *Nashville Tennessean* newspaper, a writer called for local schools to create a "customer-centric culture," to create "the loyalty and enthusiasm that is crucial to participation, funding, and community pride. The Walmart model is good for some things, but if it is quality you desire, Nordstrom is the way."

Businesses of every kind strive to become the Nordstrom of their industry. Over the years, we have collected dozens and dozens of examples of this metaphor.

Recreational Equipment Inc., a Seattle neighbor, has been called "the Nordstrom of sporting goods stores" and *Specialty Foods* magazine described A Southern Season, a store in Chapel Hill, North Carolina, as "the Nordstrom of specialty food."

A top broker for Century 21 once told *Fast Company*, "I want people to think of me as the Nordstrom of real estate."

A dean at Fullerton College in California vowed to create, "the Nordstrom of Admissions and Records."

The University of Colorado Hospital installed a baby grand piano (a popular feature in many Nordstrom full-line stores) in its lobby and began advertising itself as "The Nordstrom of Hospitals."

You can find similar comparisons in yoga studios, restaurants, cloud computing, office furniture, public libraries, construction supply distribution, hot tubs, dental offices, pet stores, thermal rolls, foundries, workplace giving, doors and windows, and contract consulting.

We've even found "the Nordstrom of garbage collection." I don't know what its return policy is, and I don't want to find out.

Even Nordstrom uses this metaphor. In describing the company's Rack division of clearance stores, Blake once said, "We like to think that the Rack is the Nordstrom of the discount world."

So, what does it mean to be the Nordstrom of your industry? It's not just a smiling face that greets you when you enter the department. It's covering every aspect of the business—the things the customers see and the things that they don't see.

How can an organization create a culture and atmosphere to provide Nordstrom-like service? This book answers those questions and shows you how to do it.

A Family Business, a Public Company

The old saying about a family business goes like this: The first generation builds it, the second generation enjoys it, and the third generation destroys it. We don't bother to mention the fourth generation because few businesses last that long.

If there was ever a family business that defies that stereotype, it is Nordstrom. Technically, Nordstrom, which was founded in 1901, is not a family business. Although Nordstrom has it's been a publicly traded company since 1971. The chairman of its board of directors is not a family member and has never worked for the company.

Nevertheless, Nordstrom is a family company in the sense that it is still run by members of the family. Brothers Blake, Pete, and Erik (who are on the board of directors), and their second cousin Jamie are the fourth generation to work in the business, which was founded by their great-grandfather, John W. Nordstrom. The Nordstrom family owns about 30 percent of the outstanding shares. In 2017, the family was exploring taking the company private.

Dollar for dollar, Nordstrom is one of the great stories in U.S. business. We may never see its like again: a century-plus-old corporation that is run by the fourth generation of a family with the same commitment to the customer experience as their forbears. With the exception of Nordstrom, the great department stores of the United States are no longer controlled or operated by the descendants of the founding merchants. Keenly aware that the challenges of modern (and future) worlds of retail are radically different from those of the world of their ancestors, this generation—like its predecessors—is continually adapting and innovating, which is why they are still around.

As of 2017, Nordstrom had 122 full-line stores in 40 states and four Canadian provinces and the Commonwealth of Puerto Rico; 221 Nordstrom Rack stores, and seven Trunk Club Clubhouses.

What Makes Nordstrom Unique?

Nordstrom's business is composed of people, product, and place. The company combines superior merchandise and motivated people to create an experience for customers that exceeds their expectations. Customers have a myriad of choices to buy apparel, footwear, cosmetics, and accessories. When they shop with Nordstrom, that's the ultimate endorsement.

The chain, which is geared toward middle- to upper-income women and men, offers attractive stores with a large, varied, and competitively priced inventory of shoes, apparel, accessories, and cosmetics, and a liberal return policy. But many stores do that—at least to varying degrees.

It's got an easy-to-use website and an active, creative social media presence. Again, a lot of companies can say that.

What makes Nordstrom unique is its culture of motivated, empowered employees, each with an entrepreneurial spirit to give great customer service. Nordstrom encourages, preaches, demands, and expects individual initiative from all employees, whether on the front lines or in support roles. Salespeople are given the freedom to create their own individual businesses, to be a franchise within a franchise. The best Nordstrom sales associates will do virtually everything they can to make sure a shopper leaves the store a satisfied customer. Nordstrom salespeople put themselves in the shoes (metaphorically speaking) of the customer. They do whatever they can to make life easier for their customers.

The qualities that Nordstrom looks for in its employees couldn't be more basic. First of all, the company wants its salespeople to be nice and motivated. You're probably asking, "What organization doesn't want to hire nice, motivated people?" The difference is that Nordstrom is dedicated to hiring people who are already nice and already motivated to do a good job—before they apply for a job.

Have you ever tried to take someone who is not nice and motivated and magically make them nice and motivated? It can't be done. And yet, so many organizations believe that—with initiatives or training or slogans or catch phrases—they can change a person's inherent nature. It can't be done. People are who they are. They are not going to change. Don't waste time and money trying to change them.

Why a Third Edition?

Through all the vagaries, vicissitudes, fads, and trends of fashion, retail, consumerism, and product delivery channels; through the existential threats of world wars, recessions, and the Great Depression, Nordstrom has survived and thrived by integrating new tools and techniques within its culture of service to offer a highly personalized customer experience that adapts to customers' changing expectations.

RSi, our consulting company, has evolved as Nordstrom has evolved. The material in this book reflects our passion and beliefs about the customer and employee experiences, and the material is the foundation of our keynotes and consulting practices.

The lessons of The Nordstrom Way are more important than ever because we are living in the age of the customer. Today's customers are the most powerful consumers in the 7,200-year history of trade among civilized societies, because they have more information, more options, better tools, and higher expectations. They want to engage with companies on their own terms, which, one hopes, translates into a seamless, painless experience across all channels.

Values

Unlike the previous versions of *The Nordstrom Way*, this edition focuses not on practices but on values. We define values as standards of behavior, the nonnegotiable beliefs that are most important in your life.

If "vision" is the head, and "mission" is the heart, then "values" are the soul of your culture. The only way an organization can create a lasting customer service culture is by hiring people who buy into the core values.

Most organizations are guided by practices that are influenced by market conditions, such as short-term strategies for product and/or service offerings. In order to stay competitive, you must adjust your way of doing business. Your organization's viability is designed by your business plan, but your longevity is determined by your personal values, which explain what you are as an organization.

"Values define who we are, and if they change we become something else," said Pete, who described practices as, "ways of doing things... that express our values. Practices may serve us well for long periods of time—but they are not values and, therefore, can be changed without changing our culture. So, if we're thinking about the business from the customers' point of view, we should evolve and be nimble and provide the goods or services that they are looking for. There are very few things that are sacred that we should stay true to. Practices, which change and evolve, deliver these values."

By adhering to a set of nonnegotiable values any organization can attract and retain the people who will help you achieve success. Once you identify the kind of people that will thrive in your organization, you will be happy only with those who share your values. We're not talking about people who think as you do, but rather people who believe as you do.

"People always ask me, how do you teach core values? The answer is, you don't," wrote James Collins, coauthor of *Built to Last: Successful Habits of Visionary Companies*, which profiles Nordstrom. "The goal is not to get people to share your core values. It's to get people who already share your core values."

And as Howard Schultz, chairman of Starbucks, said, "Culture trumps strategy. You need strategy and execution, but if you're not aligned with shared values, that is not sustainable."

Research

By way of research, we re-read the respective memoirs of members of the first three generations of the Nordstrom family:

The Immigrant in 1887 by the founder John W. Nordstrom chronicles how he left his home in Sweden at the age of 16 and arrived at Ellis Island with $5.00 in his pocket and just a few words of English. He worked his way west through a succession of backbreaking, manual labor jobs, hit a gold strike in the Alaska Yukon Gold Rush that paid him $13,000, which he invested with his friend and business partner Carl Wallin to open the modest Wallin & Nordstrom shoe store in downtown Seattle in 1901.

A Winning Team by John W.'s son Elmer Nordstrom details how Elmer and his brothers Everett and Lloyd created the biggest independent shoe retailer in the United States by the mid-1960s (and, on the side, became majority owners of the expansion Seattle Seahawks of the National Football League).

Leave It Better Than You Found It by Bruce A. Nordstrom (son of Everett) tells how he, along with his cousins John N. and James (sons of Elmer), and their cousin-in-law Jack MacMillan (son-in-law of Lloyd), expanded into apparel, cosmetics, and jewelry and created the classic full-line Nordstrom store that we are familiar with today.

Mr. John: Football, Flying, and a Proud Family Legacy by John N. Nordstrom.

We also revisited all the books that we have written about the company.

As we reviewed those books, we identified and compiled a list of the values that Nordstrom has always adhered to through four generations of family leadership.

The values we singled out are:

1. Trust
2. Respect
3. Loyalty
4. Awareness
5. Humility
6. Communication and Collaboration
7. Competition and Compensation
8. Innovation and Adaptation
9. Give Back and Have Fun

As you will see trust and respect comprise almost one third of the narrative of this book, because they are the foundation for all relationships. Without trust and respect, the remaining values are meaningless.

Nordstrom has one simple goal: to provide outstanding service every day, one customer at a time. This goal is accomplished, in the words of Blake Nordstrom, by continuing, "to improve on the little things in front of us. It doesn't sound very glamorous but that's what we're going to do."

By improving on all the little things in front of you, you will achieve your goal of providing outstanding service every day, one customer or client or patient at a time, The Nordstrom Way.

Notes to the Reader

In the course of this book, we will be citing and quoting four generations of Nordstrom. For those of you who want to keep track of the individual Nordstroms and the years that they ran the company, here is the pertinent information:

- Founder: John W. (1901 to 1926)
- Second generation: Everett, Elmer, and Lloyd (1926 to 1969)
- Third generation: Bruce, John N., and James (1969 to 1999)
- Fourth generation: Blake, Pete, Erik, and Jamie (1999 to present)

Throughout this book, we will be quoting many members of the Nordstrom family, both living and deceased. To avoid repetition, in most cases we will be using only their first names.

All quotes from Nordstrom executives come from author interviews, public speeches, and additional author research, unless otherwise specified.

All definitions of values that begin each chapter are sourced from Merriam Webster's Collegiate Dictionary, 11th Edition.

1

Trust

We have a great chance of succeeding if everyone feels that they are in an environment that trusts them.

—Blake Nordstrom

Our very existence is based on trust, which is defined as the "firm belief in the reliability, truth, ability, or strength of someone or something." We trust that the sun will rise tomorrow morning, that our car will start, that the traffic lights will work, and that our morning latte will taste exactly like yesterday morning's latte. And that's just the first hour or two of our day.

Every meaningful personal and business relationship is based on trust. The only organizations that engender loyalty and achieve longevity are those that work to earn our trust literally every day. Businesses that violate that trust will be severely—if not fatally—harmed. A trustworthy company understands that reputation is everything. Without the trust of its stakeholders—including employees, shareholders, customers, and suppliers—it may as well as turn out the lights, lock the doors, and go home.

Trust is not a strategy. Trust is how and why we live our lives—both personally and professionally. An untrustworthy person doesn't wake up one morning and say, "I think I'll try trust."

"Why do two people trust each other in the first place?" That's a question asked by Professor Paul J. Zak at Claremont Graduate University, in an article in *Harvard Business Review*, entitled "The Neuroscience of Trust." Zak, who teaches economics, psychology, and management, discovered that a brain chemical called oxytocin signals to the brains of rodents that another animal is safe to approach. In humans, oxytocin increases empathy, which is essential for collaboration.

Zak found that employees in high-trust organizations are more productive, have more energy, collaborate better, and are more loyal to their employers.

The Gallup organization, which measures employee engagement in the workplace culture, polls companies on how well they explain expectations; provide the necessary tools; and offer recognition, praise, and career development opportunities within a positive environment. When employees have a deep connection with work and colleagues, when they feel that they are making a meaningful contribution, and when they are afforded opportunities to learn and advance, then their companies enjoy superior productivity and increased profitability.

Trust Employees

Building a values-driven culture of service begins with hiring people who share those values and who fit into the culture. We then expect them to earn the trust of management, colleagues and, of course, customers, with a strong desire to give great customer service.

A college degree has never been a requirement at Nordstrom. For frontline salespeople, enthusiasm, a desire to work hard, and a capacity to generate their own traffic are much more important in a system that can best be described as a process of natural selection—a purely Darwinian survival of the fittest. As Blake has noted, "You can't teach a work ethic."

Nordstrom believes that the employee experience determines the customer experience. Its philosophy is to hire people who are attracted to the company's entrepreneurial culture and provide them with opportunities to succeed.

We believe "The Nordstrom Way" can be summed up in three sentences:

1. Stay true to the values of the culture.
2. Attract people who share the values of the culture.
3. Teach and coach based on those values.

All of that sounds deceptively simple. The challenge is to stay consistent with that humble vision so that you replenish your work-force with like-minded people. Our consulting clients often ask us how Nordstrom finds people who want to give outstanding customer service.

"Most of the time, they find us," said Bruce. "We can hire nice people and teach them to sell, but we can't hire salespeople and teach them to be nice. We believe in 'hire the smile, train the skill.'"

Nordstrom provides little in the way of a formalized training program. When asked who trains Nordstrom salespeople, Bruce answered: "Their parents." Or their grandparents or guardians—whoever instilled them with a set of values.

People will rise or fall to the expectations that the organization puts on them. If everyone in the department is chewing gum or is on the phone chatting with friends, the new hire will follow that behavior instead of engaging with the customer. But if that new hire joins a high-performance, high-expectations culture, he will either emulate that behavior and become a part of that culture or realize that this job is not for him and leave.

"Some people might think our way of doing things is too gung-ho for them," said Bruce. "Okay, then don't work here. This is not a job for clock-watchers."

High-trust companies hold their people accountable and treat them like responsible adults.

"Everything that we do is done through trust," one department manager told us. "I don't need to stand over my employees and tell them what they need to do to make the customer feel good. I trust them to make the right decision so that the customer walks out the door with a smile on her face and the purchases that help keep that smile on her face."

Managers always stress to new hires the importance of trusting their customer, and that if they are ever in doubt, they are empowered to err on the side of the customer. Slipups, blunders, or errors are not fatal at Nordstrom, where they believe that mistakes can be transformed into opportunities. When you prove your trustworthiness by promptly admitting mistakes and quickly rectifying them, you strengthen and deepen your relationships.

No Nordstrom employee will ever get into trouble for making somebody happy. They are empowered to do whatever it takes to make that happen. At Nordstrom, as long as you make the customer happy, no one has a problem with you. If you make the customer unhappy, everybody has a problem with you.

Christian Parrocco, a young Nordstrom employee, told us, "My entire career at Nordstrom has been built on trust. Every single step I've made through the company stems from trusting the people around me. We all rely on each other. When you're trusted, it makes you want to do more."

Trust from Customers

Only one out of every three existing Nordstrom customers says she has a relationship with a salesperson at Nordstrom. What's exciting for Nordstrom is that three out of four customers say that they would like to develop that kind of trusting relationship. When customers have a rapport and a bond with a Nordstrom salesperson, their spending doubles. Consider Chris Sharma, who has been the top salesperson at Nordstrom for many years. Sharma, who is a personal stylist in men's wear and furnishings in the Tysons Corner store in suburban Washington, D.C., sells in excess of $2 million in merchandise every year, and has many regular customers who annually spend between $30,000 and $50,000. That's trust.

Here's a customer letter that describes how salesperson Jackie Byrd is more than just the customer's "go-to person at Nordstrom," more than just a friend.

> She is a much-loved member of our family who just happens to work at Nordstrom. Through every major event in my relationship with my wife, Jackie has been there for me. She saved me when I needed help to remake my wife's wardrobe. She was there for me when I wanted to propose, and she helped make the entire event perfect. She was there for me when we got married. She attended our wedding, and made it perfect by simply being there. When I need her, she is always there. Always.
>
> My wife and I are expecting our first baby. Jackie was the second person we told and once we found out the sex (daughter), we drove to the mall to share the news with her first. We never considered going anywhere other than Jackie to get our unborn baby daughter taken care of.
>
> Jackie proactively seeks to meet our needs and ensure we feel loved and appreciated. I've never worked with *anyone* who has gone to so much trouble to ensure we have what we need. From driving to other Nordstrom stores to pick up an item, to bringing me dress socks to our wedding in Southern California—I don't exaggerate when I tell you Jackie is the one of top three most important women in my life. I literally could not live without her.

Nordstrom is built on people like Jackie Byrd who transcend being an employee and become loved family members.

The best Nordstrom salespeople take a long-term view of their business. It's not about making the big sale with one customer and not caring if you ever see her again. It's about developing an enduring relationship built on trust.

Elsbeth Haladay, a top seller for two decades at the Towson, Maryland, store until her retirement, understood the importance of taking the long-term view. During her first month at Nordstrom, Haladay helped a young man on a tight budget find his first business suit for an interview. Haladay made sure that he walked out of the store with complete confidence that he was dressing for success. The young man got the job, his company grew to be prosperous, and he continued to shop with Haladay. Eventually, the man became an influential public figure in the local Baltimore area, and continued his long-term relationship with her.

"The most important thing," said Haladay, "is to think about what the customer truly wants and continue to deliver that over time for an ongoing experience. Relationships are about building trust over time."

Nordstrom has many ways to develop relationships with customers. For example, for many years, Nordstrom has had a Breast Prosthesis Program, in which salespeople become Certified Prosthesis Fitters and are specially trained to fit women for all intimate apparel following a mastectomy, lumpectomy, or other reconstructive breast surgery. The program provides items and services such as breast forms for mastectomies, lumpectomies, and reconstructive breast surgery; post-mastectomy camisoles and bras; and free pocketing on any bras purchased from Nordstrom.

"The days after my mastectomy were some of my darkest," wrote a Nordstrom customer named Shana on her website TheMomEdit.com. "Words cannot express how thankful I was for the support and hand-holding Nordstrom provided to my overwhelmed self. They were able to get me out of my scratchy and stiff hospital-issued compression bra and into a silky soft Spanx contraption that was both comfortable on my scarred chest, yet still offered the binding I needed for my bruised ribs. Since none of my bras fit (seriously *none*), they also helped me select a pretty little bralette for once I no longer needed the compression." She added that her experience was so positive because of, "the caring and helpful staff at Nordstrom."

Hiring

As Nordstrom has expanded across North America, the company faces a constant challenge of finding the kind of people who want to give Nordstrom-like service, and to help them optimize their capabilities and give them opportunities so that they want to stay with the company and make it a career.

When opening a new store, Nordstrom primarily recruits from within. It draws on seasoned Nordies from throughout the company, high achievers who have grown up and learned within the Nordstrom culture. Then it hires locals to fill out the staff.

To recruit workers with disabilities, company representatives attend special job fairs and work with businesses, service agencies, and assistive technology providers that network with the disabled community.

Once a candidate has applied, he or she goes through a phone screen with a recruiter or a person in human resources, followed by in-person interviews with a department manager and a store manager. Although candidates meet with assorted members of the store team, the hiring decision ultimately lies with the department manager. Nordstrom provides managers with a variety of training tools to help them make the best hiring decisions.

For every 300 or 400 positions that Nordstrom needs to fill in a new store, the company usually receives some 3,000 to 4,000 applications. (In other words, a person has a 1 in 10 chance of getting hired at Nordstrom.) The people who are not hired are sent thank-you notes because their effort to apply is appreciated and, after all, Nordstrom would like them to remain or become Nordstrom customers.

Onboarding

New employees must buy into the culture and understand their role in maintaining and supporting the culture through their actions. On the first day of orientation, new Nordstrom employees read an introductory message that sets the tone for what is expected of them:

> As we travel along the road of life, we encounter paths that lead to a great opportunity for growth. To recognize the doors that open to a bright future is the key. Once inside, we crave support from our colleagues. We know that the health of our relationships is paramount to our own success, and that the joy of sharing ideas leads to a diversity of options. Our reward is access to a wealth of knowledge that we would have otherwise overlooked. Welcome to Nordstrom. Our door is open.

Among the paperwork that they receive is a $5^1/_2$-inch by $7^1/_2$-inch card entitled "Nordstrom Employee Handbook" (see Figure 1.1).

Welcome to Nordstrom. We're glad to have you with our company. Our number one goal is to provide outstanding customer service. Set both your personal and professional goals high. We have great confidence in your ability to achieve them, so our employee handbook is very simple. We have one rule:

OUR
ONE
RULE

USE GOOD
JUDGMENT
IN ALL SITUATIONS

Please feel free to ask your manager or Human Resources any questions at any time.

Figure 1.1 Employee Handbook

That's it. This simple, straightforward directive is the foundation upon which The Nordstrom Way is built because it removes the roadblocks to taking care of the customer.

Nordstrom believes that the more rules employees are asked to follow, the more they are separated from the customer. Such unempowered employees invariably find themselves serving the rules, not the customer. They wrap the rules around themselves like a security blanket and then send the message to the customer: "You can't hurt me. I'm protected by the rules."

Rules and policies reflect the company's perspective. Good judgment reflects the customer's perspective.

Please note: We are not talking about the rules and regulations imposed by governmental bodies and professional associations. You have no control over these mandates. We are talking about internal rules that are self-imposed. Are the rules in your organization getting in the way of how you interact with your customers? We urge you and your team to periodically revisit those rules to see if they are still relevant and important to how your organization functions.

Jim Nordstrom, cochairman of the third generation, once said, "The minute you come up with a rule you give an employee a reason to say no to a customer. That's the reason we hate rules. We don't want to give an employee a reason to say no to a customer. Our people are judged on performance, not on obedience to orders."

Nordstrom's way of doing things inspired an executive at a world famous Nordstrom vendor, who said, "At our company, we live by the rules and it's a tremendous pain in the ass. Nordstrom challenges us all to do something differently."

As you have seen, Nordstrom does not believe that great customer service emanates from lots of policies, rules, and procedures. The only way to take care of customers is to empower employees to use good judgment and focus on the issue for the customer right in front of them. The best service happens when people take ownership of their customer and do what they think is best to take care of the customer right then and right there.

"It's hard to do this without a training manual," said Erik. "We get this across by telling stories and recognizing people a lot. In the morning before our stores open, the store manager recognizes people who did a good job the day before. They'll read a letter from a customer where we've made a difference in their lives. These stories bring into reality the words that define this culture. We can't boil it down to a set of steps that everyone must go through. Our only shot at taking care of the customer is to hire the right person and empower them."

"We are going to keep making decisions that are in the best interests of the customer," said Nordstrom's chief innovation officer Geevy Thomas. "When responding to a request from a customer on the sales floor, ask yourself: 'Does this request pass the test of reasonableness?'"

How do you define "reasonable"?

After one of our RSi customer service workshops for a prominent financial services company, we were approached by an attendee, who was on crutches because her left leg had been amputated from the knee down. She told us this story:

"I would go to other department stores and ask if they would sell me one shoe. That request made them nervous and ill at ease. They would apologetically tell me that they could not do that. It was against the rules! Finally, I went to Nordstrom and asked if they would sell me one shoe. The saleswoman said, 'Absolutely,' and they charged me half the price. I'll always give Nordstrom my business."

When he heard that story, Thomas said, "When viewed from the customer with one leg's point of view, a request for one shoe at half price is a reasonable request!"

Let's say that this customer bought a $500 pair of shoes. Instead of a $500 sale, it was a $250 sale. She's told that story to untold numbers of people. We've told that story around the world. Was that gesture worth $250 in advertising? Nordstrom thinks so. That's why it empowers its salespeople to do whatever it takes to satisfy the customer.

Reinforcing the Culture

New employees become steeped in the culture. They learn the values that the company supports and the atmosphere it tries to create, where everyone is in a position to succeed. Nordstrom wants new employees to connect with the company as a whole and with their home store in particular, to help them understand what is special about their team and to get them excited about their new career.

They are schooled in the Nordstrom service philosophy and encouraged to work on enhancing the customer service experience one customer at a time.

They learn about the company's history, culture, and experience by watching video interviews with members of the Nordstrom family and top-performing employees. In person, they hear from successful store managers, department managers, and salespeople, who tell their personal stories about how they started with the company and how proud they are to be working at Nordstrom and appreciative of the opportunities they've had to prosper. So many people say, "I started with Nordstrom when I was in college. Originally it was a part-time job, but 10 years later, I'm still here." They might even shed a few tears of happiness. Sometimes people in the audience are crying along with them. This is how a generous helping of honest emotion cultivates the culture and turns what could be an abstract concept into a concrete reality.

"The most important thing I've learned is how much every single interaction with the customer counts no matter how big or small the sale is," said a salesperson. "You may not know the story behind a particular purchase. You may never know the impact that that one sale is going to have on a customer and how they view Nordstrom as a company. But if you don't make that interaction a special moment, you'll never have a chance to cultivate long-term relationships."

Nordstrom consistently reinforces this dual message: (1) every single decision the company makes is for the benefit of customers; and (2) Nordstrom employees are crucial to that experience. Nordstrom reinforces its culture with messages such as, "Our goal is to provide outstanding service every day, one customer at a time," and "We work hard to make decisions in the best interest of our customers and those serving them."

Nordstrom provides further guidance to its employees about how to achieve the Nordstrom mission in a practical way every day with a clear description of the Nordstrom culture and the things that Nordstrom values: being family; trusting each other's integrity and ability; taking the initiative (with management's support); setting and accomplishing personal goals; taking ownership; being open, honest, and respectful in communication; being a good neighbor; showing courtesy to everyone (customers and coworkers alike); and having fun. Employees learn every aspect of the company and how each aspect works and fits in with the overall culture.

"You learn from the veterans who have the culture embedded in them," said manager Callie Hutton, who started as an intern while in college. "Everyone on the team works together to train that employee, to show them how it's done at Nordstrom, how we take care of our customer. In onboarding, it's important for people to feel that they are a part of the team and that they understand our culture. People don't work for a company; they work for other people. We all have to be a servant leader for our team to make sure they feel good about working here and want to continue to work here."

Find Your Own Way

After going through employee orientation and becoming familiar with the culture, the systems, the merchandise, and the sales goals expectations, salespeople are encouraged and empowered to develop their own style, to find their own niche, their own way of taking care of business that fits their unique personality and talents because, ultimately, success at Nordstrom comes down to what works for each individual. Not everybody can be a top seller, but everybody has individual strengths.

Top salespeople are encouraged to pass on the knowledge and tricks that they have acquired along the way, such as goal setting, self-marketing, selling, using the phone, social media and, of course, customer service. That is how a customer-service, sales-oriented culture is perpetuated and sustained.

Although this book is entitled *The Nordstrom Way*, there are actually more than 72,000 Nordstrom ways, because each employee is an individual, with a unique style and approach to taking care of the customer.

"Healthy competition is good; we love to win," Nordstrom tells new hires in its company literature. "If you thrive in a high-energy, competitive, team environment, you'll love it here." (See Chapter 7: Competition and Compensation.)

Key to success is finding the right balance in rewarding individual achievement, teamwork, and customer service. Ultimately, it comes down to the individual. Nordstrom provides the information, tools, and the empowerment. Employees learn from each other and share what works. Nordstrom doesn't believe that learning The Nordstrom Way works very well in a classroom. That's why Nordstrom wants people to get out on the sales floor and learn firsthand.

Each new salesperson is matched with an experienced salesperson or manager in the same department for up to a full day of observation and practice. They work through a checklist of selling concepts and role-playing scenarios to help bridge the gap between the new hire's first day on the job and another class. Eventually, they learn the foundation of relationship selling, how to develop expert fashion knowledge, and how to confidently engage with the customer.

Top salespeople believe in making customers their best friends. Customers are there to spend money, so make them happy.

"Approaching each customer as though they would become a friend changes the way you interact with each person. Always ask yourself how you can best make the customer happy so that they'll come back to work with you again," said Elsbeth Haladay.

Empowerment

Empowerment to do the right thing is the byproduct of trust. If you boil the Nordstrom system down to its essence, down to the one sentence that separates Nordstrom from most other companies, it is this: Nordstrom gives its people on the sales floor—the front line of the business—the freedom to make entrepreneurial decisions, and management backs them on those decisions. Everything else flows from that simple premise.

That's called empowerment. In most businesses, empowerment is a cliché. At Nordstrom, it's a reality. Nordstrom empowers salespeople and managers at all levels with a wide range of responsibilities without shackling them with lots of bureaucratic guidelines that get in the way of serving the customer. Nordstrom wants its people to operate like nimble, entrepreneurial shopkeepers rather than static blocks in a retailing monolith.

"We've never tried to solve a customer service challenge at headquarters or through training modules and policies," says Erik. "We've always done it through empowerment—and that's the only way we're going to meet the challenge today."

Empowerment encourages personal ownership, which Blake called, "key to our success and our company's ability to persevere even through the toughest of times. Throughout our organization, our people are empowered to use their energy and their entrepreneurial spirit to take care of the customer. We don't have one person whose role it is to maintain the culture or manage service or our reputation. We are all responsible for keeping alive and well these components of who we are at Nordstrom."

If an employee wants to go above and beyond for a customer, or would like to make a suggestion on how to improve service or to try something new, "We want you to take the initiative," company literature says, "and we'll support your efforts to deliver exceptional service. Selling something is the best service that we can provide."

Regarding empowerment at Nordstrom, there are those who get it, those who really want to get it, and those who will never get it.

Nordstrom believes in empowering people as close to the customer as possible in order for those people to bring an entrepreneurial, proprietary attitude to their business.

As a business leader, you have to be confident enough in your system and your people to take your hands off and allow business to work.

"If everyone can feel like it's their reputation, their name on the door, and that they are in an environment that values them, trusts them, hears them, and allows them to make a difference, then collectively we have a great chance of succeeding," said Blake.

A women's apparel salesperson in New Jersey said that she approaches customer service, "as if I'm running my own shop: Greet every customer with a smile. Learn their names and keep in touch with them. Go the extra mile. A couple of times I have hand-delivered alterations to a customer's home. They were really wowed by that."

As another salesperson told us, "It may say Nordstrom on the front of the building, but I want the customer, when she thinks of Nordstrom, to think of me. I believe the department where I work is *my* franchise. Nordstrom gives you the freedom to help the customer with everything. No one tells you that there's only one way to do your business. Nordstrom lets you do whatever it takes to make the customer happy, as long as it's legal. They are not going to say 'no' to you if the end result is a happy customer."

Inverted Pyramid

Nordstrom's empowerment culture is illustrated by the company's informal structure of an Inverted Pyramid. (see Figure 1.2.) The Inverted Pyramid is a cornerstone of the Nordstrom culture.

Customers sit atop the pyramid. Beneath them are the salespeople, department managers, and executives, all the way down to the board of directors. This is both a literal and symbolic way of how the company does its business. Customers are on top because they are the most

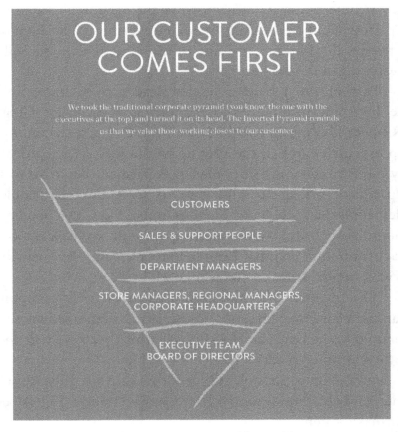

Figure 1.2 Inverted Pyramid

important. But the next most important are the salespeople because they are the ones who are closest to the customers.

"There's a lot of meaning to the Inverted Pyramid because it reflects our values," said Erik. The Inverted Pyramid guides our leadership style, which is about support, not command-and-control."

It is the job of the rest of the workforce to help those people on the sales floor (the front lines) because they are the engines that power the machine. If they aren't making money, then the company isn't making money.

As employees rise up through the managerial and buying ranks, they are referred to as "moving down the pyramid," "supporting" their departments, and providing "servant leadership." This kind of language buttresses the Nordstrom value of humility, which we will discuss in greater detail in Chapter 5.

"Part of my job as a servant leader is to serve my team up the Inverted Pyramid," said regional store manager Greg Holland. "Respect flows from the bottom of the Inverted Pyramid [where the top executives are] all the way up to the top. As a regional manager, my job is to serve my store managers because they have to serve their department managers, who have to serve our salespeople and our salespeople have to serve our customer. I ask the people I support questions such as: 'What's getting in your way? What is the thing that's frustrating you that I can help to alleviate?' I get my kicks out of serving others. It makes me feel good."

"The Inverted Pyramid lends itself to the trust component," said manager Adrienne Hixon. "Those of us farther down the Inverted Pyramid know our marching orders, which is to support those closest to the customer. That's a huge trust factor."

Smart people can look at Nordstrom's Inverted Pyramid "and scoff at it," said chief innovation officer Geevy Thomas. "Those people will not make it here."

Trust Among Customers

Treat each customer as a whole person, as an individual, so that you learn their likes and dislikes. When customer service comes from the heart, individual salespeople can add their own personal touch in order to create a relationship in which the customer feels as if she is working with a friend. The result is a strong connection that turns a happy customer into a brand ambassador.

No matter how electronically wired we are, there will never be a substitute for personal interaction for creating long-lasting relationships. According to a global study from IBM, 67 percent of members of Generation Z shop in brick-and-mortar stores "most of the time," with another 31 percent shopping in-store "sometimes." In other words, 98 percent of Gen Z shops in-store at some time or another, and they still expect a personalized experience.

What a priceless way to connect with your customers! The brick-and-mortar experience will never die because we are all social animals. Retail is where the economic order and the social order meet. And what says "instant gratification" more eloquently than brick-and-mortar stores? You can buy an item and immediately have it in your hands. What a concept!

Most shoppers say that in-store purchase decisions are influenced by store associates whom they seek out for help or recommendations. These shoppers say that they are more likely to make a purchase from a sales associate who has helped them in the past. Sales associates who remember customers' personal preferences have a positive effect on how much they buy.

Van Mensah, a men's suit salesman at the Pentagon City, Virginia store, is a native of Ghana who holds an MBA degree from Northeastern University in Boston. He believes that honesty and sincerity are the keys to success.

"When you are dealing with the kind of clients who come to Nordstrom, if you try to play games, they will see through that very quickly," he said. "If you know the merchandise is not right, come forward and say, 'in my professional opinion, this is not going to work for what you are buying it for.' You might lose some money; it might be the most expensive item he wants to buy. But I would rather sell him something that is less expensive but will actually work better for him. If you tell him the product is not right for him, you get more credibility."

When you've established trust, customers will give you the benefit of the doubt.

"The moment of truth is what happens between salespeople and customers," said Pete. "So, every decision we make—based on every experience we have had—must go back to supporting the relationship between the salespeople and the customers."

Front-line people are empowered to establish relationships with customers and to find ways to take care of them. They must be able to listen to the customer, understand their needs, and follow through to fulfill them. If a salesperson can't find an item that a customer has requested, Nordstrom insists that the salesperson gets back to that customer to engender trust and loyalty. Customers want to do business with a company—and an individual—they can trust.

Nordstrom is faced with the challenges of reinventing itself while preserving cross-generational appeal. For a department store that's been around since 1901, Nordstrom faces a two-headed challenge: to not alienate its aging-but-existing, bread-and-butter base of loyal customers, while at the same time, being sufficiently hip and relevant to attract new, young customers. You don't want people to think you're stodgy and old, but you don't want to exclude those over 30, either.

What remains constant is that Nordstrom looks at every change and initiative through the lens of the customer.

Return Policy

One such customer-friendly approach is the Nordstrom return policy, which is a virtually unconditional, no-questions-asked money-back guarantee. (Due to public health laws, there are some product category exceptions, such as cosmetics.)

This generous policy was established in the 1920s, when Nordstrom consisted of one shoe store in downtown Seattle and one near the campus of the University of Washington, a few miles away. After all, shoes are one purchase that can be confirmed only by use—walking around to make sure they fit. Brothers Everett, Elmer, and Lloyd of the second generation dreaded having to deal with obviously outrageous or unreasonable returns, so, they reckoned, if they could pass off the responsibilities for the adjustments and complaints, their enterprise would be more personally enjoyable.

"We decided to let the clerks make the adjustments, so they would be the fair-haired boys," recalled Elmer. "We told them, 'If the customer is not pleased and comes to us, we'll give her what she wants, anyway.'"

Tracking the costs for the first year, they found that they could afford the return policy, which became a point of differentiation from their competition. In a world where most retailers make returns an ordeal, Nordstrom made the experience as painless as possible, which generated priceless word-of-mouth advertising. It still does.

The third generation of Nordstroms—Bruce, John N., and Jim—preserved and encouraged that generous approach to returns.

Returns, Jim told us in the early 1990s, "are the best way in the world for us to own the customer forever. When somebody comes in with a return, that's the time to separate yourself from the competition. You have to remember that the person who's returning the item is back in our store. We want them to see that we're on their side."

Jim believed in greeting that customer with a big smile and that, "If you take back the item with a smile and no questions asked and the customer walks out the door happy, what's that worth? A lot. It's the best sales closure we have as a company. What a wonderful opportunity for a salesperson to own a customer."

A retired jewelry salesperson in southern California agreed: "Our return policy is a wonderful way to establish trust with the customer. The first part of my approach to returns is to have a 'yes' attitude, which is even better than a positive attitude. If you smile and are genuinely helpful, the customer can see you're not just here for the money. Each customer encounter—whether it's a return or a sale—is an opportunity to build trust. When you sell something to a customer, you make a commission. But when you make a friend, you create a lifetime relationship."

Jamie Nordstrom, who is Jim's son, said simply, "We don't have a return policy. What we have is a belief in empowering our salespeople to deliver the best service. The best person to make a decision on how to best serve that customer—including taking returns—is the person standing right in front of the customer."

The company's overall primary message is: "If you're ever in doubt as to what to do in a situation, always make a decision that favors the customer before the company."

If a customer comes into the store with a pair of five-year-old shoes and complains that the shoes are worn out and wants her money back, a Nordstrom employee has the right to use her judgment to give the customer her money back.

Empowering the people on the sales floor with the freedom to accept returned merchandise is the most noticeable illustration of the Nordstrom culture, because it is the one that most obviously affects the public.

Nordstrom has its liberal return policy "not because we're good guys; we do it because it works," said Bruce. "We want to do more business. It serves our purpose to be nice to people, to wait on them, to turn the other cheek."

Doesn't that unconditional policy invite abuse? Sure it does, but central to the Nordstrom philosophy is a desire not to punish the many for the dishonesty of a few. Which is not to say that returns are often frustrating for Nordstrom salespeople. You have the customer who "borrows" a dress for a couple of years (or a weekend) and then returns it. Nordstrom will put its foot down in egregious situations.

"Now, if somebody goes too far, we'll say that although fairness is our credo and that's how we try to live our retail life, this adjustment is not fair," said Bruce. "The ones we say 'no' to are people who have a lengthy history of wearing something and then returning it."

Because it is a multichannel retailer, Nordstrom allows customers to return to their stores any items purchased at nordstromrack.com or its HauteLook online site, where luxury brands are sold for up to 75 percent off the original price. This move alone has driven millions of incremental trips to Rack stores.

"Customers would rather just walk in a store and hand us this stuff than box it up and wait for UPS to pick it up," said Erik. "We can do that because we have stores. It's good for the customer and it happens to be good for us. We like to have customers in our stores because they tend to buy something. That's why we need to focus on what's important to the customer. With online returns to the store, the best thing you can do is to get that return done as quickly as possible. That's a great experience. That's the best way to get them excited about spending more time in the store."

Nordstrom's return policy also means that the company stands behind what it sells, essentially telling the customer, "I am so confident you are going to love this item, I want you to buy it, wear it to work someday, and if you do not feel great about it, I want you to bring it back," said Jamie. "I don't want you to have anything in your closet that you bought from Nordstrom that you do not love."

Everett, of the second generation, was a perfectionist about product quality. Once, an order of women's pumps was found to be poorly constructed. The uppers were separating from the soles near the ball of the foot. When Everett alerted the manufacturer, he was told, "They're not all bad. Just send back the ones that come apart." Everett's reaction was to go into the stockroom, take every pair of shoes from that manufacturer and start popping them apart, just to make sure that no customer would have a problem.

Quality Center

Ensuring highest product quality continues to be essential to the Nordstrom culture. In an industrial/retail area south of Seattle is the Nordstrom Quality Center, which is dedicated to making sure that the products the company sells will be of the highest quality and workmanship.

From throughout the company, the facility receives defective shoes and clothing that can be repaired. Quality Center employees sort all of an individual vendor's merchandise into one bin, then invite the vendor's representative (or, in some cases, the principal of the company) to the facility to show that individual what common quality issues Nordstrom is facing with the company's merchandise, such as buttons that are poorly sewn on. Nordstrom offers feedback on how construction problems could be solved. Vendors that want to continue to sell to Nordstrom are grateful for the feedback.

The Quality Center has also helped Nordstrom to solve one of its historically major concerns dating back to its strictly shoe store days: matching up the shoes that had lost their mates. That task was virtually impossible to do in individual stores, because, in the natural course of business, some shoes bought for one store might get transferred or returned to another store within the company.

The Quality Center refurbishes and shines up mismated shoes as well as shoes that were worn and returned by customers. The spruced-up shoes are marked down and then sent to Rack stores.

Typical of Nordstrom, most of the workers at the Quality Center are veteran employees who have worked on the sales floor, so they are familiar with merchandise construction and know what to look for.

★ ★ ★

As counterintuitive as it may sound, the return policy works to the benefit of the best salespeople, who realize that returns are part of the game. They take back the returns with a smile, knowing that many of those customers will return. Some enterprising Nordstrom salespeople will even send a thank-you note to a customer who has returned a purchase. If you were that customer, wouldn't a gesture like that get your attention?

More than 67 percent of customers who shop at Nordstrom.com return unwanted items to a Nordstrom store—even though the company does not charge postage and handling for returns. Stores are convenient, and the shopper actually has real, live, knowledgeable salespeople to work with. The salespeople are motivated because the customer is generally a ready buyer.

This is why taking a multichannel approach has been so effective for Nordstrom. We will go more deeply into multichannel in Chapter 8: Innovation and Adaptation.

The Tire Story

The most famous Nordstrom return story (which the national press frequently cites) is the tale of the salesperson who gladly took back a set of automobile tires and gave the customer a refund. What doesn't ring true about this story? Nordstrom has never sold tires. Is the story apocryphal?

No—it's true! In 1975, Nordstrom acquired three stores in Alaska from the Northern Commercial Company, a full-line department store that sold many products, including tires. (Northern Commercial was the local B. F. Goodrich dealer.) After Nordstrom bought the stores, the company converted them to Nordstrom stores and eliminated lots of departments, including the tire store across the street, which Nordstrom later stocked with menswear and shoes.

Here's how John N. described the scene:

> I was visiting Fairbanks soon after the change [from Northern Commercial to Nordstrom] and was standing in the back of the store with our manager. The doors opened for the day and we saw a small, older man walking across the street carrying a tire. He entered the store and looked around, seemingly confused. Our manager started toward the door and I grabbed him and said, "Let's stay here and see how our team handles this."
>
> Our young salesman greeted the customer and asked to help him. The little guy said he had purchased the tire here and it didn't fit his car, so he wanted to return it. I was so happy when our young salesman asked if the customer remembered how much he had paid for it. The guy thought it was about $25. Our guy opened the cash register and handed him the $25 and told him he hoped he would return so we could help him with clothing or shoes.
>
> We took the tire and nailed it up in the stockroom as an example of how you give customer service. We didn't realize the story would become a wonderful cultural pillar of the company.

This has become the quintessential Nordstrom return story, and one hears variations of it all over the United States. When we speak to corporate groups, the number one question (there is no close number two) they ask is: "Is the tire story true?"

"We have to create new stories every day," said Geevy Thomas. "We want to know what your tire story is from yesterday. What are we doing today to *wow* the customer?"

As we've seen, Nordstrom places trust for all parties concerned above all else. Trust is fragile. It is a value that has to be reinforced every day in as many ways as possible. Nordstrom has made it a priority to maintain that trust as best as it can. That's not easy, with more than 72,000 employees across North America and Puerto Rico. But the company continues to prove that an approach and philosophy that constantly emphasizes, recognizes, illustrates, and rewards the value of trust has created a foundation for loyalty and longevity.

2

Respect

Our frontline people don't work for us; we work for them.
Our job is to support them in their job.

—James F. Nordstrom

Respect is defined as "a feeling of deep admiration for someone or something elicited by their abilities, qualities, or achievements." Isn't that what every business desires?

Robert Spector grew up working in his father's butcher shop, Spector's Meat Market, in Perth Amboy, New Jersey. As a young boy, he would occasionally accompany his father, Fred, to the abattoirs, where he would find himself standing in a large walk-in meat freezer with his dad and his dad's suppliers. Even though Robert couldn't have verbalized it at the time, he could sense that these suppliers respected his father. (Of course, it helped that Fred Spector paid his bills on time.) It was clear to Robert that respect was essential to conducting business.

The best companies are generous with their respect—for colleagues, vendors and, of course, customers.

Does everyone in your organization have respect for their colleagues? Do they appreciate the unique role each individual plays in their collective success? That's the essence of teamwork. Sometimes in competitive sports and in business, there are teammates who might not necessarily like or love each other, but who nevertheless respect each other's contributions, which enables them to work together for the greater good.

We once gave a full-day program to people who worked in the supply chain department of a major health care organization. Our material is presented in plain English. Most of our slides have just one simple sentence. Nevertheless, at one point, the department head, who had arranged the program, said to us, "Do you think you could dumb down your presentation for this audience?" Dumb down? All we could think of is: "If this is what you think of the people you hired, what does that say about you?" Clearly, this person did not respect the rank-and-file employees.

This cavalier attitude was reinforced by the head of the department when he introduced us to the frontline employees that we were working with, for what was going to be a four-hour training session. This session was on a Saturday, which meant that the employees were there on their day off. The department head stepped up to a lectern in the front of the meeting room and told the employees what a great session they were about to take part in, and how much they were going to learn. And then he added: "Unfortunately, I won't be a part of this today because I have to go back home to renovate my kitchen."

Where was the respect? Certainly not for the frontline workers who sacrificed to be there.

Compare that approach to that of Harry Home, a retired, long-time Nordstrom manager. "I always sold the premise to new employees: You are not good because you are at Nordstrom. You are at Nordstrom because you are good."

Throughout all of its changes, Nordstrom's foundation of service remains the same. It's based on having a motivated, energetic, empowered person dealing directly with the customer. Those kinds of people are what best define Nordstrom, its reputation, and its ability to survive and thrive.

Inspirational leaders never ask a staff member to do something they wouldn't do themselves. Jim said it best: "Be the kind of boss that you would want to work for."

Back in the mid-twentieth century, while making buying decisions at the New York wholesale shoe markets, Everett of the second generation encouraged young buyers to develop their own ideas and make their own decisions. After the sales representative of a women's shoe vendor showed the company's line to both Everett and a young Nordstrom buyer, the rep asked Everett for his reaction. "Don't talk to me," said Everett, "Talk to my buyer." The sales rep then turned his eyes toward the nervous 22-year-old buyer and asked him for his opinion. After that, the employee became a true, dedicated Nordy, who rose up through the organization. Once that young buyer felt that he had earned the respect of the estimable man known as "Mr. Everett," he felt that he could accomplish anything. That's powerful.

Respect for the Culture

In the Nordstrom culture, talented individuals develop personally as well as professionally. By investing in the whole person, Nordstrom retains employees and builds teams to lead growth, expansion, and innovation.

Like every other value at Nordstrom, respect for the culture includes storytelling, which plays a critical role in spreading Nordstrom's values and priorities throughout every level, department, and region. Reflecting the company's Inverted Pyramid, Nordstrom's philosophy is that neither "corporate" nor "leadership" creates the Nordstrom story; employees and customers do.

Stories of customer service and teamwork above and beyond the call of duty have their own word at Nordstrom: "heroics."

Heroics demonstrate and illustrate qualities of teamwork and customer service that ultimately produce sales. Heroics pass on the company's cultural values to fellow employees, and serve as reminders of the level of service to which all Nordies should aspire or surpass. Heroics also allow team members to recognize their colleagues for the special lengths they went for a customer.

When a Nordstrom employee witnesses a coworker providing great service—whether for a customer or a colleague—he or she is encouraged to write up what that coworker did and submit it to the department manager or store manager, who will publicly praise that employee. The best stories are shared through as many internal corporate communication channels as possible.

There are many examples, such as the manager in the men's suiting department, who sent a tailor to a customer's office when he heard the customer was unhappy with his suit. Or the member of the house-keeping staff who found a customer's bag and airline ticket in the store parking lot, contacted the customer, and drove to the airport to return what she had lost.

By sharing these heroics, management honors and salutes employees who go above and beyond the call of duty, which sends the message that customer service—both internally and externally—is what makes Nordstrom Nordstrom.

"Make sure all heroics are fussed over in front of everybody in store meetings," John N., the founder, wrote in his book. "Bring the person to the front and have them stand slightly in front of you while you brag about them. Everybody in the room will love it. Next time it may be them!"

Most frontline workers get it. They understand that the people who run Nordstrom single out, honor, and reward outstanding acts of customer service. Consequently, they know that one sure way to advance in the company is to give great customer service. If you see a great example, you're going to imitate that example because you work in an organization that encourages such behavior.

Here's an illustration of instantly transferring the culture to new associates: At the then-recently opened Nordstrom store in Richmond, Virginia, a woman, who had been shopping elsewhere in the mall, walked into Nordstrom with large, cumbersome packages and boxes and asked a couple of young, new male Nordstrom employees if they would help her take the items to her car. The two Nordies happily honored her request. A reporter for the *Richmond Times-Dispatch*, who witnessed this scene, asked the employees why they seized the opportunity to help a woman who had not bought those items in their store. Their answer: "This is Nordstrom." Enough said.

Respecting Colleagues

Every Nordstrom manager understands the challenges of the sales floor because they have all been there, done that. They understand that the way to nurture the career paths of the frontline people that they are supporting is to empower them to take care of customers and colleagues. Managers are there to be a listening board, to give advice, and to answer questions.

The best store managers embody the Nordstrom culture and perpetuate that culture by developing their own individual mentoring programs based on the individual needs of the frontline people that they support. Although this is not a one-size-fits-all approach, support always includes praising colleagues, recognizing their accomplishments at every opportunity, and rewarding them for a job well done.

One often-overlooked element of empowerment is encouraging new hires to observe, take notes, and ask questions.

"Over the years, we've done more and more mentoring for people at the entry level," said Bruce. "Newcomers get a quick understanding of what we're trying to do, but some of them don't buy into it. If you lay it out for them, via a mentor, the people who have it within themselves are more apt to buy into our deal."

Inspirational mentors transfer that culture to new Nordstrom associates. That's how this company has been able to thrive for more than a century, through four generations of management. Literally every Nordstrom employee we have spoken to over more than three decades can point to at least one significant mentor in his or her career.

"I have three mentors who I talk with regularly," said manager Callie Hutton. "They play a big part in my decision making. When I have issues, I call them and ask how I should deal with those issues. It's important to have that kind of relationship with other people in the company, so you can bounce ideas off of them because they've gone through it and seen it."

Buyers and department managers (and vendors) regularly ask salespeople for their opinions on merchandise because salespeople are touching the product and seeing the reaction from a broad cross-section of customers, many of whom they know well. Menswear personal stylist Chris Sharma regularly relays customer feedback to the buyers because, as he said, "When you run a business, you have to do that. You can't wait for walk-up business. I always make sure I know what I have on the floor and what I need from the buyer. If I don't see anything that I want to sell, I always call the buyer and ask what's coming in. What's available in this month and next month? Then I can communicate with my customers and tell them when I will have things coming in for them."

Respecting Customers

Nordstrom does not follow a strategy built around price, process, brand, technology, or any other corporate tactic or buzzword. Everything Nordstrom does is viewed through the lens of the customer—and how it can improve the customer experience. Every aspect of the Nordstrom experience starts and stops with the customer. When it comes to exploring new ways of improving its service and results, Nordstrom asks itself one simple but profound question: What would the customer want?

Does your organization start every initiative and every discussion with that question? If not, why not?

Nordstrom's philosophy is to adapt to the wants and needs of the customer in order to ensure that the Nordstrom system works for the benefit of the customer. The customer is the one who drives the business. That's the ultimate show of respect.

"We stand where the customer stands," said a top salesperson in a women's sportswear department in the Midwest. "We're on the floor where the customer is. And we strive to serve one customer at a time."

"Selling clothes isn't what we do," said a retired Nordstrom executive. "It's filling people's needs and making them feel better emotionally."

Bob Bender, a retired senior executive who worked very closely with the third generation of Nordstroms, told us, "We learned early on that you have to show respect to your product, your customer, and to every part of your business. When we brought that shoe out to the customer, it was tissued right, and it showed you had respect for the merchandise. The Nordstroms believed that there was a lot of money in those boxes."

This focus on the customer is emphasized and reemphasized and re-reemphasized at each and every opportunity—including in its annual report to shareholders, which always opens with this salutation: "Dear Customers, Employees, and Shareholders." Note the order of importance. Nordstrom believes that taking care of the customers and employees ultimately benefits the shareholders (which include management, employees, and customers).

Nordstrom's respect for customers begins not just when the doors open in the morning but even before the doors open. Even though Nordstrom officially opens at 10 A.M., the retailer actually opens its doors at 9:50. Why would it do that? Because it wants to show customers that Nordstrom values customers' time. If a customer arrives 10 minutes early, Nordstrom doesn't want the customer to have to wait outside for the store to open. That small gesture satisfies an unexpressed need. Customers don't know that they need it—until they do. Again, it's a small gesture, but it speaks volumes and it's an experience that a customer will not soon forget. After all, retail is detail.

In today's business world, Nordstrom thinks only about what customers expect in their shopping experience. Convenience is paramount for today's time-crunched customers. Whatever kind of experience the customer wants on that particular day, Nordstrom just wants to make it perfect. On any given day, a customer might want a three-minute experience; on another day, she might want a three-hour experience. When you're flexible, you are serving the customer on her terms. Nordstrom is continually work on improving the speed and convenience of its customer service. "How much time do you have?" is the best opening question you can ask a customer.

Nordstrom is constantly speeding up its process of accepting returns to just a few painless minutes. Customers asked for this courtesy. Nordstrom responded. That initiative is good for the customers because it gives them back the time they had expected to lose. And the initiative is good for Nordstrom because that gift of time puts most customers in a positive frame of mind to shop while they are in the store. As Adam Smith, the eighteenth century moral philosopher and economist aptly observed, "it is not from the benevolence of the butcher, the brewer, or the baker that we expect our dinner, but from their regard to their own interest." Smith was not criticizing these shopkeepers, but merely stating a universal truth.

Respect begins when Nordstrom customers are small children. When working with a child who's trying on footwear, a top salesperson advises, "Talk directly to the kid. Make the kid feel good. Don't talk to the parent. The parent wants you to show respect to their kid. If we do a good job of making that kid feel good, it translates into so many other things, mainly sales."

Imagine that you're five years old and a grown-up is talking directly to you and wants to know what you think. If you don't believe that such a public display of respect means something special, then you don't remember what it's like to be a kid.

Beyond Sales

Sometimes, customer service has nothing to do with selling things to the customer. Here are a few examples:

A customer contacted her Nordstrom salesperson in Tacoma after the customer had gotten a botched hair coloring at a salon. The salesperson called her own hair stylist and booked the customer in for an appointment the next day. "The true sign of a person who has their client's best interest at heart is going the extra mile to help without any expected return," wrote the customer.

A customer, who was traveling in France, was out of money, her ATM card was not working, she had no place to stay and nothing to eat. The customer contacted her credit card companies, hoping they would temporarily increase her line of credit. None were willing to help her. She contacted Nordstrom and spoke to Kristi, a telephone customer service specialist. Without hesitation, Kristi increased the customer's line of credit so that she would be able to afford food and lodging until her flight back home. The customer said that Kristi took care of her "like family."

A female customer was driving past the Salem Mall in Oregon on her way home. She heard a noise from her car but kept on going. When she arrived home, she examined her car and discovered that one of her hubcaps had fallen off. She figured it happened when she was driving past the mall. She couldn't get over there right away, so she called the Nordstrom in the Salem Mall, told the operator what had happened, and asked if a store employee could venture out onto the road to see if the hubcap was there. This being Nordstrom, an employee did just that. He found the hubcap, brought it back to the store, washed it, and notified the customer, who came in to pick it up.

"We love that story," said Pete, "because it means people don't just think of Nordstrom for buying things, they think of us as a place where they can find solutions."

Two employees from the store in Chandler Fashion Center in Chandler, Arizona, went above and beyond for some customers on their special day. One of the salesperson's personal customers was planning a surprise wedding, full of special touches for his fiancée, in her best friend's backyard. Everything from the invitations to the photographer was falling into place—except for somebody to perform the ceremony.

As the day of the wedding drew near, the customer went to his Nordstrom salesperson to have his tuxedo fitted—and it came up in conversation that the salesperson was an ordained minister.

"Does that mean that you could marry us?" the customer asked.

The salesperson said yes.

His department manager happily gave him the time off. The wedding was a success, and the customer's bride was cheerfully surprised. The salesperson held up very well under the pressure of meeting family and friends for the first time at the wedding. And the department manager, who is also an artist and owner of his own gallery, invited the happy couple to the gallery to pick out a wedding present. The couple continues to frequent the store as they live happily ever after.

Recognition

Neuroscience indicates that recognition has the biggest influence on trust, "when it occurs immediately after a goal has been met; when it comes from peers; and when it's tangible, unexpected, personal, and public," according to professor Paul J. Zak's *Harvard Business Review* article on "The Neuroscience of Trust." Zak adds, "Public recognition not only uses the power of the crowd to celebrate successes, but also inspires others to aim for excellence."

Nordstrom believes it is essential to publicly and privately express recognition and praise for a job well done.

"There are two things people want more than sex and money," Mary Kay Ash, founder of Mary Kay Cosmetics, has said. "Those two things are recognition and praise."

A Nordstrom store manager told us that, "Recognition and praise are the best motivators I know. When you recognize and praise your people, they will go out and do anything for you. Every time you talk to me you're going to hear me talk about my team and how wonderful they are and what they did. We have so many good folks who have made a career of this, and it's up to us to provide them some uplift as they work day after day, week after week, year after year. We put people in front of their peers and tell them that they are the kind of person we want others to emulate. We tell them that we value and cherish their input to this company, and we wouldn't be as successful without that individual. That's strong stuff."

Recognition is powerful, as long as it's authentic and specific. Whatever their level on the Inverted Pyramid, employees want to feel needed and valued.

"We are at our best when we recognize good performance," Bruce wrote in his memoir *Leave It Better Than You Found It*. "Why are we constantly finding ways to praise and recognize our people? Because selling is tough. Sometimes you're dealing with angry and complaining customers who are yelling at you. Believe me, I know from experience."

Seven times a year, each region has Recognition Meetings to achieve what Bruce referred to. Showing employees that the leadership cares is a powerful way to reinforce the values and principles of the Nordstrom Way.

These meetings are buoyant affairs that begin at 8:00 in the morning. Upbeat music blares over the speaker system and colleagues hug each other like long-lost friends. The energy is infectious. Some people bring pom-poms, clappers, flags, and even bullhorns to create a celebratory atmosphere.

Each store in the region has its own nickname, hashtag, and slogan. For example, the store in Tacoma ("T-town") chose as its slogan, "There will be service."

An observer can't help but get caught up in the spirit of the event, which is almost like a pageant. While the surface objective is to recognize employees, individual stores, and departments for sales increases and promotional ideas that drive sales increases, the meeting is also used to rally the troops and to get everyone excited about the performance of their teammates in their department, their store, their region, and their company. Cash awards are given to individuals, departments, and stores.

To promote the opportunities for advancement within the company, employees see a PowerPoint slide on how many people have been promoted and to which positions. Employees are shown the career path of a Nordstrom leader, who's brought up on stage, to show others how they got to where they are today. These top employees serve as inspiration for newcomers: "Be like her. Do what he does."

Recognition Meetings are not exclusively about sales. Employees are selected as "Customer Service All Stars." They are nominated by their peers because they represent Nordstrom values such as reputation, drive, curiosity, honesty, and integrity.

At one Recognition Meeting we attended, Charlie MacDonald, who worked in the menswear department at a Nordstrom store in north Seattle, was selected as an All Star. This is what his manager and coworkers said about him:

"When we think of an All Star, Charlie is the first name that comes to mind. He is a role model and a team player on the floor. His ability to not only think about his own metrics, but those of the total department, helps him be influential in making the day."

"Charlie's customer service is like no other. His customers trust and respect his opinion, and he creates strong relationships with them. When people shop with Charlie, they feel like they are shopping with a friend. His commitment to our customers and building relationships sets the bar for the entire store."

"He constantly thrives to better himself and is happy to help others. He is driven and self-motivated, takes initiative, and is open to feedback. His positive attitude and energy are infectious. He is here every day to work hard and make customers happy."

It's recognition and praise like that that motivates Nordstrom employees to do their best.

Nordstrom also recognizes the efforts of people in support positions such as alterations, housekeeping, and logistics, to let them know, in the words of a Nordstrom manager, that "We do notice."

Customers' letters of appreciation are read, and positive achievements are recognized, while coworkers stand up and cheer for each other.

Adding emotional drama to the proceedings, All Stars are not told in advance that they are being honored. However, Nordstrom does notify their parents and/or spouse and children, whom Nordstrom secretly sneaks into the meeting—unbeknownst to the honoree. Imagine that you are an honoree. You are called out of the audience and you bound up to the front of the room for a standing ovation in front of your peers. Then from stage left, you see Mom and Dad or Grandma and

Grandpa and your spouse or significant other and kids, who are sharing this emotional moment with you and then pose with you for pictures. We've witnessed this scene many times. It never loses its power to inspire and motivate.

All Stars are given a 33 percent store discount (rather than the traditional 20 percent) for one year, special business cards recognizing their achievement, and an All Star pin to wear. Their photos are displayed in the Customer Service department of their store for the next year, as well as on the company's internal website. They also get the work shift that works best for them. Some prefer the busiest times; others opt for shifts that coordinate with their personal lives.

"It's important that we single people out for their extra efforts," said Blake. "There is no better way to enhance our culture than to put a person who has gone above and beyond, who has used good judgment and taken care of their customer, on a pedestal in front of their peers."

These morale boosters double as pep rallies. The people who attend these meetings get charged up and take that energy back to their departments.

But pep rallies can go only so far. "You can have all the pep rallies in the world, but the best motivation is stocking the right item in the right size at the right price," Jim once said, "There's nothing more demoralizing for a salesperson than to not be able to satisfy the customer. Our number one responsibility to our salespeople is to have the products that the customers want when the customers come into the store."

A good Recognition Meeting encompasses four key aspects:

1. Sincere appreciation for the people being honored and detailing what makes these individuals valuable.
2. Team spirit so that people feel that they work for a company that appreciates their efforts.

3. Teach people something new, such as sales techniques or promotional ideas. Show motivational videos, skits, and performances.
4. Perpetuate the culture—and each team member's place in the culture. Reinforce what makes the culture unique.

At RSi's keynote presentations and workshops, we ask members of the audience to think of one coworker they would like to recognize and thank for a job well done. We're looking for a simple, heartfelt acknowledgment for being a reliable and valued member of the team. If the person they'd like to thank is not in the room, we entreat them to say thanks when they get back to the office.

We also ask if someone in the audience would like to thank a coworker who's also in the audience. When one person publicly thanks a colleague in front of everyone, it's a powerful moment that neither will ever forget. That is respect.

3

NORDSTROM

Loyalty

Some companies demand loyalty from personnel, but we felt that loyalty should first come from us to them. Loyalty is something earned, not expected.

—Elmer Nordstrom

Loyalty is a feeling of strong support for someone or something. We all crave it and once we have established loyalty we nurture it, because loyalty, like truth and respect, can be lost in the blink of an eye.

Loyalty—to customers, colleagues, vendors, and community—is the by-product of respect, recognition, and reward for a job well done. Loyalty helps to create a bond and allegiance that enables us to get through the inevitable challenging times. The only way people will be loyal to an organization is if they are shown appreciation, given respect, and rewarded with good pay and a piece of the action.

Because brothers Everett, Elmer, and Lloyd of the second generation of Nordstroms believed that the commitment to loyalty started with them, they dedicated themselves to providing opportunities for their employees to make more money than any other retail salespeople in Seattle.

"We did everything we could to get the best people, and once we had them, we did everything we could to keep them," said Elmer. From as far back as the 1930s, Elmer and his brothers believed in promoting from within, which is a Nordstrom employment practice that endures to this day. (We will be discussing Nordstrom's promote-from-within policy in several other sections of this book.) "We wanted our people to know that they could work their way up, while also learning about the business on different levels," Elmer said.

A Career or a Launching Pad

You can't buy loyalty and job satisfaction. You can rent them, but you can't buy them. Golden handcuffs (benefits and/or deferred payments that an employer provides in order to discourage an employee from leaving) might be an effective short-term solution, but that approach is less effective over the long term. Many good people will sacrifice dollars for a place that values and trusts them.

That's not to say that money doesn't matter. Nordstrom instituted profit sharing back in 1952 because the brothers wanted to make sure that their employees who had done a great job would have money for retirement beyond Social Security.

"It was a natural development that reflected our basic philosophy: The better we treated our people, the better our people performed," recalled Elmer.

Nordstrom believes that its employee profit-sharing plan helps it attract better personnel who see themselves as part owners of the company. (We go into more detail on profit sharing in Chapter 7: Competition and Compensation.) Profit sharing sparks motivation and encourages allegiance to a company where individuals can see the potential of building a career. Over the course of our research, including countless interviews with Nordstrom employees, we heard many stories of individuals initially joining Nordstrom for a summer job or part-time job while they were getting their higher education, but who then chose to stay because of the career opportunities and the potential to make a very nice living and to retire in comfort and security.

Nordstrom management understands that it's imperative to find career advancement opportunities and other ways to keep bright, talented, motivated people.

"I don't think we would have blossomed if we didn't grow," said Erik. "People wouldn't have seen the opportunities and would not have stayed. There are lots of examples of people who have had great careers with this company. They started on the selling floor and grew with the company. They are the ones who are responsible for our reputation."

Adrienne Hixon, a store manager who has worked for Nordstrom since 1992, told us that she "grew up on the sales floor." Starting as a seasonal cashier because she needed a job, "I was going to stay here until I got my 'real' job," she said. "I'm still here."

The company nurtures the development of employees and offers a "My Career" website and ongoing coaching feedback.

"We view career development as a shared responsibility among managers, employees, and the company," said Pete. "Our approach is to enable our leaders to be the teachers as well as the developers of their people's growth."

Nordstrom feels that even people who don't make a career with the company can benefit from working there. Over the course of our research, we've met people who worked at Nordstrom for a period of time, learned valuable lessons, and went on to careers in law, real estate, sales, and virtually every kind of field you can imagine.

Pete recalled the time he was asked to discuss career choices with a young woman starting out in the business world.

> I told her that even if you don't know exactly what you want to do, Nordstrom is a good place to work, because if you can come here and understand what it's like to interact with customers and do that well, then this experience is going to benefit you in some way. It's going to look good on your resume if you spent some time here and did well. Every company has a customer orientation to it. We're fortunate to be known for that. So use that to your advantage. Learn something here. Do the best you can at it, and let it take you where it takes you.

Diversity

Nordstrom salespeople come from all walks of life.

"Our people don't have one look, one background, one culture," says Erik. "The common thread is they are themselves. They are genuine."

Nordstrom recruits through targeted media, job fairs, community organizations, and college placement centers. The company reaches out to communities in which it operates to recruit, employ, train, and promote ethnic and racial minorities in its general employee and management ranks. It has historically been ranked among the "50 Best Companies for Minorities" in the United States by *Fortune* magazine.

As of 2017, of the company's total employment of approximately 72,000 people, 51 percent were people of color and 70 percent were women. It is among the top 50 companies in the United States based on wages of women corporate officers, and women constitute more than 40 percent of its corporate officers.

"What makes this thing work is that it is such a diverse group of people, with all these different experiences," said Blake. "I believe we are the sum of our experiences. How do you hire people with those elements and also get different points of view? That's the challenge. We have to be reflective of our communities and our customer base. We need to encourage different styles and points of view."

Nordstrom is considered the first upscale retailer to advertise in *Ebony*, a magazine that caters to African Americans. It also advertises in other publications targeted to people of color, including *Asian Enterprise Magazine*, *Minority Business News USA*, *Hispanic Business*, *Black Enterprise*, and *Ability*.

Nordstrom regularly features models that reflect the population's various ages, races, and disabilities, which is "really about reflecting the customers and communities we serve," said a company spokesperson. "We serve diverse customers, and it's an opportunity for them to see themselves when they're looking through our print catalog or online. We don't promote it or go out and talk about it. We just think they look great."

Leadership Model _____

In addition to its concentration on service and people, Nordstrom focuses on leadership development, which is grounded in experiences. The best leaders at Nordstrom are the ones with the most diverse experiences, the most mentors, and the most ups and downs. Adversity is a great teacher.

"The biggest learning comes from the toughest experiences," said Blake. "We used to be prideful of our silo approach: You start in the shoe stockroom, you sell shoes, you become a shoe department manager or a shoe buyer. You're a specialist in shoes. Today, our people move to different departments and different parts of the country and get to work with and learn from different people. That kind of experience creates a much better leader."

Steve Wilkos, winner of the company's highest honor—the John W. Nordstrom Award—tells new employees: "Try to learn a little bit from a lot of different people. Sometimes we get too locked in working for a certain leader or particular division. You don't get well rounded that way. I believe the more people you can work for at Nordstrom, the better off you'll be. Your career at Nordstrom is yours to build. There are no rules.

"That's a tough concept for a lot of people to understand. Most people miss it because they're looking for this big magical system. It's not there. At Nordstrom, you come in, be yourself, take care of the customer, and have some fun. If you can do that, you can do anything you want in this company." Wilkos's philosophy is summed up by the sign-off he uses on his e-mails: "Smile. Have Fun. Sell Stuff."

The John W. Nordstrom Award is bestowed on the manager who best exemplifies the characteristics of the founder, which the company lists as, "hard work, persistence, servant leadership, loyalty, honesty, ethics competitive spirit, and an unwavering commitment to putting the customer first."

John W.'s great-grandsons Blake, Pete, Erik, and Jamie, solicit nominations from regional managers, who in turn request them from store managers. Generating good sales numbers is one major criterion, but the winner must also be a selfless team player and committed to doing business the Nordstrom Way.

The identity of the winner is known only to the handful of people who will keep it a surprise until it's announced at a regularly scheduled regional Recognition Meeting.

Nordstrom likes to add a little drama to the proceedings for maximum impact. While the regional manager is conducting the meeting, all of a sudden the Nordstrom family members make their surprise entrance. The employees erupt as if the Beatles had just shown up because everybody knows that something special is about to happen. The Nordstroms announce the winner—who is taken completely by surprise. The winner springs up to the front of the room, and suddenly here comes his or her spouse and children (who have been notified in advance) to share the moment. Tears and laughter abound.

Each year, the new and past winners of the John W. Nordstrom Award attend a dinner in Seattle, hosted by the Nordstrom family. The company pays for the travel and lodging for the winners and their guests—even if those past honorees are no longer working for the company. Now that's loyalty.

Best Places to Work

Nordstrom has been ranked among *Fortune* magazine's "100 Best Companies to Work For" every year since the list was first published in 1998. In the most recent survey, Nordstrom was the third-oldest firm, trailing only Goldman Sachs and American Express. It is also one of the 25 most-admired companies in the United States, according to *Fortune*. It is one of only five companies to make *Fortune*'s "Best Companies to Work For" and "Most Admired" every year the survey has been taken.

The company is one of *Fortune's* "100 Best Workplaces for Millennials." According to one millennial frontline salesperson: "This is the first retail establishment that I've worked for where supervisors above my managers have taken an interest in my well-being and performance. Management tries their best to make sure new hires feel welcome by maintaining their open door policy and always being available for anyone, whenever they need to talk."

Every year Nordstrom scores a perfect 100 percent on the Human Rights Campaign's annual Corporate Equality Index (CEI) survey, which rates large U.S. employers on their policies, practices, and benefits related to gay, lesbian, bisexual, and transgender communities and employees, recognizing the company for creating a workplace that is committed to equality for gay, lesbian, bisexual, and transgender employees.

Some salespeople who work at Nordstrom may find that they are in the wrong job. If selling is not their strong suit but they like working for the company, Nordstrom will find a place for them in a nonsales position. They don't want to lose people who have been with the company for several years, because such people understand the culture and can be valuable team players.

A (Bob) Love Story

You might not be aware of who Bob Love is, but old-time fans of the Chicago Bulls of the National Basketball Association will tell you that before there was Michael Jordan, there was Bob Love. Love was a star forward for the team from the mid-1960s to the mid-1970s, and was the team's all-time leading scorer, until Jordan. (Love is still third, behind Jordan's teammate Scottie Pippen.)

Love, who grew up in poverty in rural Louisiana, finished his NBA career in 1977 with the Seattle SuperSonics. After a debilitating back injury, financial problems, and the breakup of his marriage, he had almost hit rock bottom. Adding to his difficulties was a severe stutter, which made it difficult to find a job. In the 1980s, he got a job busing tables and washing dishes at the restaurant in the downtown Seattle Nordstrom store, at $4.45 an hour. It was hard to miss a 6-foot 8-inch African American busboy. When he was recognized, people would whisper, "Hey, that's Bob Love. What a shame."

This is how Love described what happened next, in his book *The Bob Love Story*:

> About a year after I started working, John N. Nordstrom approached me. [He said] "We think you could have a future with our company, and we'd like to help you get your life together. But first you'll have to do something about your speech. If you're willing to try we'll pay for it." At first, I couldn't believe what he'd said. It was the opportunity I'd been waiting for. It seemed as though the weight of the world had suddenly been lifted from my shoulders. It had been years since anyone had shown that kind of personal interest in me. For the first time since I was a child and my grandmother had taken care of me, I felt that someone was concerned about me as an individual. It didn't have anything to do with basketball or being an athlete, it was about me as a human being.

After trying to work with several speech therapists, Love finally found a woman who could reach him. Part of his therapy was speaking in front of groups, which he had never done before. It worked. After several promotions in Nordstrom's food services division, Love eventually left Nordstrom and was hired by the Chicago Bulls as the team's goodwill ambassador, representing the organization at various functions throughout the Chicago community. To this day, he makes more than 300 appearances a year at schools, charity events, basketball clinics, and nonprofit agencies, and is an honorary spokesperson for the National Stuttering Federation of America.

The depth of his loyalty and appreciation to Nordstrom cannot be measured.

Customer Loyalty/Sell a Relationship

Until he retired in 2000 after almost three decades, Patrick McCarthy was the quintessential Nordstrom employee. For the last 25 of those years, McCarthy sold men's tailored clothing in the downtown Seattle flagship store and was number one in sales throughout the chain for an astonishing 15 years in a row.

An entrepreneurial self-starter, like all top Nordstrom salespeople, McCarthy, who considered himself "a franchise within a franchise," was, in his day, one of the best-known salesmen in Seattle. He drew from a personal client list of 7,000 people, ranging from recent college graduates to chief executive officers to United States senators.

McCarthy used to tell the story of playing golf one day with a couple of people who didn't know who he was. At the first tee, one stranger who was in his foursome asked the standard getting-to-know-you question: "What do you do for a living?"

To which McCarthy replied: "I sell a relationship."

The questioner flashed a quizzical look, and then returned to the golf game. But at the second hole, he had to ask the question again: "No, really, what do you do for a living?"

McCarthy replied: "I sell men's suits at Nordstrom."

"Oh, so that's what you do," said the stranger, fully satisfied with the answer.

"No," McCarthy replied. "That's not what I do. What I do is sell a relationship."

And that's exactly what all successful businesses and salespeople do—sell relationships.

"It's not easy to attract a new customer and it's not easy to keep them," said regional manager Greg Holland. "You earn your business one customer at a time."

It is axiomatic that people like to do business with people they like. If your product or service is similar to your competitor's, and the price for that product or service is similar to that of your competitor, what will be the reason why you get the business and not your competitor? The answer to that question is the relationship you have with your customer and the trust you have built up over time. Once you've established and nurtured that relationship and never take it for granted, why should your customer go anywhere else?

Nordstrom is constantly reinforcing the value of relationships to its sales force because a loyal customer invariably goes back to the same salesperson. That's how you build your business—by being trustworthy, reliable, keeping your promises, and making adjustments along the way as conditions change.

"A lot of times, salespeople are in a rush to make a quick sale," said clothing salesman Van Mensah. "But a quick sale is not nearly as valuable as a long-term relationship. If a customer is looking for a specific item, you do everything possible to find it for him. I don't think I'm providing the customer with good service unless I exhaust all the avenues within the company to satisfy the customer's needs. That extra effort is going to sustain your business in the long run."

Customer Loyalty to a Salesperson

Customer loyalty is the coin of the realm in business. Nordstrom salespeople generate that loyalty by taking ownership of the customer and the customer experience. But what's even more remarkable about the Nordstrom culture is how customers feel about Nordstrom salespeople.

In our consulting practice, when we speak to clients, invariably someone in the audience will come up after our presentation and open the conversation by saying, "I have this Nordstrom salesman," and proceed to tell a story about outstanding customer service—either one spectacular example or just a description of a good, solid, steady, loyal relationship that has grown over the course of several years.

In most sales cultures, salespeople are always claiming a customer as their own. But when a customer claims a salesperson as his or her own, that's powerful; that's a relationship. That's loyalty.

Pat McCarthy saw that loyalty firsthand when he was mentored by his role model, a Nordstrom salesman named Ray Black. Black was a professional men's clothing salesman, thoroughly knowledgeable about the merchandise. Before joining Nordstrom, Black had worked for many years in several of downtown Seattle's finest specialty menswear shops, and his loyal clients followed him from store to store. "They came into the department asking for Ray because he identified their needs and knew how to satisfy them," said McCarthy. "If Ray wasn't working that day, those clients would turn around and leave. They only wanted Ray to work with them. Men saw him as an ally. They heeded his advice on where to get a good haircut or what style of glasses to wear. Their wives saw Ray as the mediator who could interpret their views to their husbands."

Every transaction, every touch point, is an opportunity to create a meaningful moment, an emotional connection that will endure—a *relationship*. Therefore, in every customer interaction, you and your team must consider these three questions:

1. Am I enhancing the customer experience in a meaningful way?
2. Am I creating loyalty by satisfying the customer?
3. Am I contributing to the financial health of our organization?

The answer to each one of these questions must always be a resounding "Yes!"

Stories of Loyalty

Do you know one small gesture that can make a huge difference in your business relationships? Remembering the customer's name. That small but meaningful touch gives customers the feeling that they are important and that their business is valued. According to Nordstrom, of all the questions the company asks its customers, the one that most highly correlates with how much money they spend is: "Does the salesperson remember me from my last visit?"

A top seller in a women's department in California remarked, "As simple as it sounds, it's very important to look the customer in the eye and call her by name. Then you need to learn her style and her size. When she comes back, you can pull her size right away and say, 'These jeans should fit you perfectly.'"

That kind of service engenders loyalty.

"Loyalty is why I fly in [to Phoenix] from Santa Fe, New Mexico, twice a month to get products," wrote a customer about a salesperson named Thomas. "Loyalty is never hesitating on where I'm going to shop for a new pair of shoes, or a Michele watch for my better half, or even those custom shirts that you all make for me that fit so perfectly. Loyalty, in a world of many options, does not come easy and is very hard to learn. I commend Thomas for solidifying my loyalty to Nordstrom."

One saleswoman studies the travel schedule of a good customer who often travels to Europe, "so I could schedule her alterations appointments or find a dress for a special event or a new suit if she was meeting with a foreign dignitary," said the saleswoman.

"We believe with every fiber of our being that our customers are smart," said chief innovation officer Geevy Thomas. "You can't fool them on pricing. We have a sign in the employee area of The Rack: 'Our customers are not loyal. They expect the best product at the best price every day.' They want us to win, but if somebody else has the same dress for a dollar less, they are going to buy it there. We should have no delusions about that. We have to earn the business every day."

Twenty percent of customers are members of Nordstrom's loyalty program, and that 20 percent accounts for about 40 percent of the sales. Loyalty program members "visit" (go to the store, log in, text, or call) Nordstrom twice as much as nonmembers and spend three times as much money.

Responding to customers' requests, Nordstrom continually works on offering a more personalized, flexible, and inclusive loyalty program that allows customers to earn points to get exclusive perks including private shopping parties and early access to sales, regardless of how they choose to pay for their purchases—whether through Nordstrom credit, store cards, or outside credit cards.

★ ★ ★

Robert Spector has his own story about valuing the loyalty of customers. As a young man, Robert, like his grandfather, father, mother, uncle, sisters, and cousins worked in their family butcher shop in a farmers' market in Perth Amboy, New Jersey. Robert went to college in Lancaster, Pennsylvania, which is about a three-hour drive from Perth Amboy. One Saturday, toward the end of Robert's senior year, he was back in Jersey, working behind the counter at his dad's shop.

A long-time customer said, "Robert, I hear you're about to graduate college."

"Yes, I am," said Robert.

"You should thank me," said the customer.

Robert looked at the customer quizzically, wondering what he meant. The customer saw that Robert was puzzled, and proceeded to explain his statement: "I've been a loyal customer of your dad's for 25 years. I paid for your college education."

To that, Robert had a simple, two-word response: "Thank you!"

That brought home the message that every customer is valuable—not just for the business that they are giving you today, but for all the business they are giving you over the course of a lifetime, based on trust, respect, and loyalty.

Vendor Loyalty

At Nordstrom, the importance of relationships and loyalty extends to its vendors.

Many of Nordstrom's relationship "secrets" are actually old-fashioned ways of doing business. The second generation of Everett, Elmer, and Lloyd weren't just working hard in their stores; they were also cultivating relationships with their vendors in the shoe industry.

"We built rapport with our suppliers and treated their representatives with common courtesy," said Elmer. "For instance, we always believed that when a traveling salesman came to town, they should be entertained by us and not the other way around. We would pick up the tab in restaurants and quite often invited salesmen to our homes for dinner. Our families reported that they looked forward to these dinner guests."

Bruce has fond childhood memories of his dad Everett bringing home traveling salesmen and manufacturer representatives for dinner and drinks.

"If we had had a larger house, we probably would have let them sleep there," said Bruce. "We got to know these salesmen well. My sister Anne and I looked forward to one particular salesman coming to our house because he always brought us big all-day sucker lollipops."

The loyalty that the Nordstroms developed with their vendors helped them during the Word War II years, when the supply of leather was tightly controlled. Domestic footwear production was allocated primarily for military use, and retailers were rationed a quota of shoes that they could sell. Once they reached their daily quota, many other Seattle shoe stores closed for the day. The Nordstrom brothers did the contrary.

"I vividly remember the specific days during the course of the year when ration stamps came due and customers were allowed to use them to buy a pair of shoes," recalled Bruce. "There were so many people lined up, waiting to get into our store that the fire department would allow in only a certain number of people at one time. The customers would literally buy everything we had."

Because Nordstrom paid its suppliers in advance, the company was able to get its hands on many pairs of shoes when its competitors couldn't. Because it was usually offered the right of first refusal on available merchandise, Nordstrom earned a reputation for being a store that was well stocked. By the end of World War II, Nordstrom became the largest independent shoe store in the United States and one of the largest in the world in terms of square footage and volume.

Vendors continue to play an active role in the business, all the way to the selling floor. Nordstrom wants vendors to have relationships with salespeople and department managers to help with presentation and product knowledge. Nordstrom holds its vendors accountable. Product is everything. Loyalty is required; it's not optional.

"Nordstrom wanted to find a way to recognize the people who do it the best; people who not only make the best products but are honest and ethical and really a pleasure to be partners with; people who care about our success and people whose success we care about," said Bruce.

Nordstrom reciprocates its loyalty and appreciation to vendors with a special recognition. Every year since 1992, Nordstrom selects several companies from more than 30,000 of its vendors to receive its Partners in Excellence Award to recognize the invaluable role vendors play in helping to create the best possible shopping experience. To be chosen, a vendor must be customer-centric and consistently demonstrate a commitment to quality, value, service, partnership, and business ethics.

Over the years, these honorees have included relatively new companies as well as long-standing ones such as Estée Lauder, Nike, Ralph Lauren, Tommy Bahama, Hugo Boss, Josie Natori, and UGGs shoes.

Nordstrom is well known for taking a chance on a vendor, nurturing that relationship, and helping that vendor grow—not only within Nordstrom, but also within the retail industry.

One example is the shoe company named for its founder, Steve Madden, who told *Women's Wear Daily*, "There would not be a Steve Madden brand without Nordstrom. They allow entrepreneurs like myself to have a national base."

When Nordstrom talks with vendors, the big question is, "How can we do more together?"

Brands covet an invitation to win shelf space at Nordstrom. When Madden was first asked to attend a Nordstrom buyer's meeting, "It was like an invite to the White House," he said.

4

Awareness

I learned to be more sensitive to what was happening around me, to notice what was hot and what was not, to be aware of what worked and what didn't work. In order to run their own business, all of our entrepreneurial salespeople must have that level of awareness.

—Bruce Nordstrom

Awareness is the state or condition of having knowledge and consciousness—two qualities that are essential to creating a memorable service experience.

In his 1950 memoir, founder John W. Nordstrom recalled the very first day of business for his little shoe store, which he opened in 1901 in downtown Seattle with Carl F. Wallin, whom John W. knew from their days in the Klondike during the Alaska Gold Rush. Wallin's previous business experience had been the running of a 10-foot-wide shoe repair shop in downtown Seattle. John W. wrote:

> I had never fitted a pair of shoes or sold anything in my life, but I was depending on Mr. Wallin's meager knowledge of shoe salesmanship to help me out. Well, this opening day we had not had a customer by noon, so my partner went to lunch. He had not been gone but a few minutes when our first customer, a woman, came in for a pair of shoes she had seen in the window. I was nervous and could not find the style she had picked out in our stock. I was just about ready to give up when I decided to [let her] try on the pair from the window, the only pair we had of that style. I'll never know if it was the right size, but the customer bought them anyway.

Opening day sales totaled $12.50.

What is important about the story of Wallin & Nordstrom's first sale is that John W., without even realizing it, hit on one of the foundations of the Nordstrom Way that continues to this day: Do not let a woman leave the store without selling her a pair of shoes.

Besides that, he established a culture whose cornerstone is: "Do whatever it takes to take care of the customer." Ever since 1901, the same principle applies because Nordstrom looks for people who demonstrate a keen awareness of the wants, needs, and tastes of each and every individual customer.

John W. was in the store every day, listening to what customers liked and disliked about the quality, fit, and style of the shoes. He would write down that information on a piece of paper and put it into his suit pocket to remind himself of what to have in his store to satisfy his customers and keep them loyal.

On a daily basis, the Nordstrom culture demonstrates, encourages, and reminds every team member in every part of the organization to "put yourself in the shoes of the customer." The best salespeople have a high level of awareness, combined with curiosity and a desire to help you find just what you're looking for.

Awareness is impossible to achieve without experience. Because they've been there before, seasoned, empathetic employees know how to react to virtually everything that the customer is experiencing or reacting to. Consequently, canny Nordies can recognize (and adjust to) positive and negative signals and cues.

Because they are unencumbered by a lot or rules, Nordstrom salespeople are free to use their awareness and best judgment in each individual customer interaction. Again, this is the shining Nordstrom example of empowerment.

"You learn to live in the gray area at Nordstrom," said a salesperson. "You must look at each situation with new eyes and make sure you respond to the individual needs of the issue right in front of you instead of applying a cookie-cutter solution. Living with ambiguity at

Nordstrom can be challenging, but in the end it keeps our responses to people and issues very real."

Imagine hiring employees who are comfortable with ambiguity. These are the kind of people who can evaluate situations and make speedy decisions. Wouldn't you like a whole team of those people?

Betsy Sanders, a former top Nordstrom executive and a former member of the board of directors of Walmart Stores, remembered the day when she was managing a women's apparel department in a Seattle-area Nordstrom store, and she saw Bruce, John N., and Jim of the third generation coming through the store on their way to a meeting on real estate matters. She noticed that Bruce had a look of consternation on his face. He motioned toward Sanders and pointed to two women who were leaving the store, complaining that, "they were never so disappointed in their lives." Bruce asked Betsy to find out what had happened.

"I thought, 'Wow, this is what Nordstrom is all about.' It's about the chief executive officer about to go into an important real estate meeting and yet still caring about what was happening on the sales floor," Sanders recalled. "I went over to these women and explained to them that Mr. Nordstrom had overheard what they had said and was very worried that we had disappointed them. They started to laugh. They said, 'We wish you could do something for us. We've got champagne tastes but a beer income.' They had fallen in love with a dress in one of the departments but they couldn't afford it. I said that I might be able to help them."

Sanders brought the customers over to a more moderately priced department and eventually sold them each two dresses, which cost less than the one dress they had first admired.

But that's not the end of the story. Several hours later, the Nordstroms came out of their meeting, "looking bedraggled," Sanders continued. "Bruce came over to me and said, 'Betsy, I know you took care of those customers. I just want to hear what the story was.' That was just emblazoned on me. I thought, 'My gosh, the customer really is number one with them.' It didn't matter what was on his mind. He was not going to forget there is a customer with a need."

Awareness on the sales floor must be a constant. Although it's important to pick up on what the customer is wearing, veteran Nordstrom salespeople caution that snap judgments based on a customer's appearance can cause you to lose out on a potentially lucrative sale. For example, a woman once walked into the sportswear department of the Nordstrom store in Tacoma. She was in her fifties, dressed in tacky clothes and a pair of old white tennis shoes, one of which had a hole in the toe. She did not look the part of a Nordstrom customer, and no salespeople rushed over to her. After a few minutes went by, Pat McCarthy, a new salesman at the time, came over to say hello. Two hours later, she had purchased about $25,000 worth of sport coats, shirts, and, sweaters, which, she explained, were uniforms for the crew of her boat. She turned out to be the daughter of a famous American industrialist, and she was on her way to her estate in the San Juan Islands, north of Seattle.

The cliché, "Don't judge a book by its cover," was never more apropos.

"We talk with our team all the time about floor awareness," said manager Callie Hutton. "We should be aware of what's happening in our store. Make sure you know who's on your floor and how you are going to help them. Have your head up so that you can greet and engage a customer. You should be aware of what's happening outside our store. Is there a parade or a political demonstration? What holiday is coming up? With a regular customer, are you aware of who's in their family, and their network? Our customer service culture is to get to know you as a person. It helps us sell to you. But we're also your friends. My customers are my friends because I've gotten to know their lives so well."

It's important to be aware of the competition and what they're doing in terms of merchandise, technology, and so on. What are they doing that you're not doing?

"We are never so cocky to think that we are doing it the best way and that we couldn't be better," said executive Greg Holland. "That awareness and curiosity is important for a company to continue to grow."

"Heads-Up" Service

The pace is rarely leisurely at Nordstrom Rack, which is the company's discount store division. The Rack's playbook is to be "sized, filled in, clean, and clutter free with a fast and friendly checkout." The Rack is stuffed to the gills with merchandise, which customers (who are shopping on their own) keep unfolding and misplacing, which means that Nordstrom employees are in a perpetual state of refolding and relocating. But they still have to be aware in order to help customers who want to pay for their items and get out as quickly as possible using mobile checkout. In order to meet that challenge, Geevy Thomas, former Rack president, said, "we went from 'heads-down' service, which is about sizing; to 'heads-up' service. People on the floor must have their heads on a swivel to see the customers, be aware of what needs they might have, and what opportunities we have to take care of them."

Managers' Roles

Managers create, maintain, and support the corporate service culture. Therefore, they must have an appreciation and awareness of the company's history, culture, guiding principles, trials and tribulations, failures, and successes.

Senior managers' responsibilities include hiring the right people, then empowering, managing, mentoring, praising, rewarding, and retaining those people. They create the atmosphere and the culture, but it is up to the people on the front lines to do the rest.

Because they have experienced every level of the organization, frontline managers know what to look for in a new hire, and they know how to empower those people, mentor them, recognize them, and praise them for a job well done. Rather than sit behind a desk, managers are expected to spend some of their time on the selling floor (like the proprietors of small boutiques) interacting with the customers and the sales staff. They are paid a salary plus commission on any sales they make and are eligible for a bonus tied to percentage increases in sales over the previous year.

The store manager's primary responsibility is to set the tone for what happens on the sales floor, interacting with the salespeople and the customers.

"Much of what happens in this company is environmental," said a manager from the East Coast. "You absorb it by watching and seeing the focus and priorities, and it snowballs."

A Nordstrom store manager in the Pacific Northwest said that part of her job is to promote an attitude among store employees that reflects: "It's not 'this is my department and that's your department.' It's 'this is our store, our customer, our results.'"

A store manager in the Pacific Northwest makes sure that he knows the names and the faces of everybody who works in his store. "Being able to praise people is so important. It's the simple, personal things you say about them. You walk up to a salesperson and you say, 'I saw you had a 15 percent increase yesterday. Good job!' That's powerful. You need to point out to others what makes that person a unique member of his or her department."

Making Memories

"Every time a customer comes into our stores is an opportunity to create a memory," says a store manager." We need to staff our store with memory makers."

Here are a few examples of how aware and mindful Nordstrom salespeople created memories.

After purchasing a prom dress for her 16-year-old daughter, a mother went to the shoe department to find matching shoes. She mentioned to a saleswoman that her daughter walks with crutches and wears braces on her feet that go halfway up her shin. She always had to wear "ugly, clunky" shoes to formal affairs. The saleswoman encouraged the mother to return to the store with her daughter and she promised that she would find the perfect shoe for the teenager. A few days later, when mother and daughter returned, the saleswoman brought out a shoe that matched perfectly. The saleswoman "tried it on her like she was Cinderella," wrote the mother in a letter to Nordstrom management. "It fit!!!!!!"

The daughter, mother, and saleswoman discussed whether to have a shoemaker add a bit of "insurance" (a strap or tie) to make sure the shoe would stay on. The saleswoman suggested that if they added a strap, they could hide it with a bow. As the mother and daughter were leaving, the saleswoman asked them to return with a picture of the girl at the prom, which they did.

When customers perceive associates less as salespeople and more as problem solvers, those associates become more powerful ambassadors for the brand they represent.

A Nordstrom customer from the East Coast wrote this story to the company: "I am deaf, and I wanted slippers for my mother. I left the old slippers in my other car." The Nordstrom salesperson called the woman's husband for her (she couldn't use the phone), "got the size, and talked him into shopping for dinner and cooking it."

A husband and wife from New Hampshire were shopping at a Nordstrom store in the Midwest. A salesperson (let's call her Jane) was helping them. The wife tried on a red jacket with matching sweater and looked fabulous. Her husband kept telling her to buy them, but she hesitated even though she loved them. Jane questioned the customer about her hesitation. The customer told her they were in from out of town for a party, and she hadn't brought her jewelry. Jane asked whether the customer liked the necklace and earrings that Jane herself was wearing, and the customer replied 'yes.' Jane offered to loan them for the evening. The customer bought the jacket and sweater and when Jane wrapped the purchases she also wrapped her jewelry to go with them. The couple was staying close to where Jane's son works, so she gave them directions to drop off her jewelry with him. The jewelry was returned along with a very gracious thank-you note.

During a Nordstrom anniversary sale one July, a Nordstrom store provided golf carts to carry customers and their packages to their cars and provide transportation to the store from the other side of the mall.

On a hot and humid afternoon, one Nordstrom golf cart driver named Joyce was heading back to the store to recharge her cart when she noticed a customer in distress. The customer had many packages and had forgotten where she parked. Joyce offered to help the customer find her car. As they drove around the parking garage, the customer remembered the car was one level up. Joyce began making her way up the ramp, but the cart's power went out and it couldn't make it up the incline. The customer tried to help push, but Joyce would not hear of it. She told the customer, "Oh no, we're Nordstrom, please have a seat and I will push the cart." So in her skirt and heels, Joyce pushed the cart, the customer, and her packages to the top of the ramp. Once on level ground, Joyce was able to get enough power to deliver the customer to her car.

How about this one? Two Canadian shoppers were visiting the downtown Seattle store. As one of them was trying on a pair of boots and looking at them in the mirror, a thief swiped her purse and her other shopping bags. The purse contained all her Canadian money, ID, iPhone, and car keys.

The shoe salesperson contacted security and the store manager, who accompanied the two women to an in-store Nordstrom restaurant to wait for the police. Magically, a restaurant server materialized with chocolates. For the next four hours, the server brought the two damsels in distress two full meals, drinks, more chocolates, and a bottle of bubbly to take back home to Canada.

After filling out the police report (and learning that the thief's picture was caught on security cameras), the shopper and her friend still needed to get back home. The store manager had a solution. He hired a locksmith to make the shopper a replacement car key so that she and her friend could drive back to Canada. Oh, and the manager gave her $400 in cash and took her to pick out a new purse—compliments of Nordstrom.

Please note: great customer service doesn't have to be those kinds of grand gestures. It can be just as powerful when it's a small, human kindness.

Christine Virtue, a customer who has a Christian ministry with her husband, Brian, posted a Nordstrom experience she had with her young daughter, Morgan, who has special needs.

"Lately I have been dealing with multiple school systems, physical therapists, occupational therapists, and doctors who all specialize in working with children and more often than not I have left more hurt, sad, frustrated, or misunderstood," she wrote. "Then I go to Nordstrom. And they of all people 'get it.'"

Morgan, who has cerebral palsy, wears a brace on her lower leg, so her parents must buy her two pairs of the same shoe, two sizes apart. At Nordstrom, the salesperson told the parents that they could buy the shoes that Morgan liked in the two different sizes. The salesperson was empowered by Nordstrom to break up the pairs of shoes so that each fit the proper foot—and charge just the price of one pair. That is standard Nordstrom policy for any fitting discrepancy over a size-and-a-half. As Morgan's mom wrote:

> Literally tears sprang to my eyes as Morgan and I picked out really cute shoes that she could wear. We have been going to Nordstrom for Morgan's shoes ever since. We left feeling special not because of Morgan's needs, but because of the way we are treated. Nordstrom is committed to serving its customers and they demonstrate consistently an awareness of what it's like to be the customer or client. They treat us in ways that reinforce for my daughter that her brace and cerebral palsy don't have to define her and in ways that speak to me as a parent and say, "We get it, we want to make life a little easier for you."

When a customer came to the Nordstrom store in the Stanford Shopping Center in Palo Alto, California, to purchase a handbag, salesperson Jennifer Youkhanna showed the customer options both online and in the store. The customer chose a bag in black that was on sale and an exclusive of the Anniversary Sale. The bag was available online and was to be directly shipped to the customer's home.

Unfortunately, the customer later received an e-mail from Nordstrom indicating that her order was cancelled because it could not be fulfilled. She was disappointed. But the following day the customer got a call from Jennifer Youkhanna, who apologized that the order had been cancelled. But she also had good news. She had just received a bag on the sales floor that was exactly the one that the customer had ordered. Sold! If Jennifer had not been aware of the progress of the order and the problem in ordering, she never would have made the sale nor impressed her customer.

Measure Both Feet

Asked about the best advice he gives his shoe salespeople, Bruce Nordstrom replied: "I tell them to measure both feet."

Measure both feet? In the literal sense, a knowledgeable shoe salesperson will measure both feet because she knows that a customer's right foot might be a slightly different size than the left foot. So, by measuring both feet, she is showing the customer that she's a professional, that she knows what she's doing. Nordstrom people are trained to understand the nature and anatomy of the foot, in order to insure the best fit.

Just as important as the actual measurement is the salesperson's taking the time to talk to the customer and to begin planting the seeds of a relationship by asking pertinent questions:

What kind of business are you in?
Are you on your feet all day?
Do you need dress shoes or more casual shoes?
Do you play sports?
Do you need shoes for those activities?
Do you have foot problems?

All the while, that salesperson is creating a relationship by taking note of what the customer is telling her. The salesperson is using his product knowledge and awareness of trends to make a connection with the customer and to sell more merchandise. And every successful salesperson knows that the customer has all the answers. All you have to do is ask—and be aware of their answers.

Everyone Is in Customer Service

When everyone on your team is aware of the importance of taking care of the customer, then everyone on your team is in the customer service department.

Take the manager in the restaurant in Nordstrom's downtown San Francisco store, who saw a young boy spill blackberry lemonade on his entire sweater. Aware that the weather was cold and that the boy and his mother were about to go walking to see a play after lunch, the manager brought the boy a new sweater to wear and took the soiled sweater (that wasn't from Nordstrom) to alterations to be cleaned.

Or how about this one from a customer from Tucson, Arizona, who was with her 14-year old son and 47 other kids on a school trip to Los Angeles, which included a formal banquet dinner and a concert by the Los Angeles Philharmonic Orchestra that night. The mom had forgotten to pack her son's dress pants. After finding out there was no way to ship his pants there in time, she called Nordstrom's store in Topanga, California, early in the morning before it opened. Ramon Lopez (assistant manager in Logistics), took the call and said he would find someone in the clothing department to help the mom once the store opened. As the mom wrote:

> Mr. Lopez himself called me back shortly before 10:00 A.M. and got information regarding my son's size, the type of pants, and color. He worked with the store's Kids' World Assistant Manager Norma Arias, who looked for the type of item that I needed.

Mr. Lopez found out the store had only a size 18 available at that moment, so he arranged for the pants to be altered. Mr. Lopez put Ms. Arias on the phone with me, and she took down my payment information. I didn't have to re-explain everything to her; Mr. Lopez had already apprised her of my situation.

Just in case my son needed it, Mr. Lopez included a belt in my order. To top this all off, on his way home from work yesterday, Mr. Lopez hand-delivered the pants to the hotel where my son and his classmates are staying, getting them there a couple of hours before the banquet dinner. He even called me once they were delivered so I'd know they got there in time. It was a load off my mind since my son was so worried about not having dress slacks for the evening. You have a customer for life in me, not to mention my son.

The Diamond Story

Here's a story that encapsulates all the values we've discussed thus far: trust, respect, communication and collaboration, and awareness.

Lisa McIntire Shaw was shopping at the Nordstrom store at the South Park Mall in Charlotte, North Carolina. It was near closing time. She tried on some clothes, made some purchases, and went directly home. That night, before going to bed, she discovered that a 2.8-carat diamond from her wedding ring was missing. She assumed that she lost the diamond at Nordstrom.

The very next morning, Mrs. Shaw went to the store when it opened and headed over to the women's department, where she had last been. She got down on her hands and knees, searching for the diamond.

Eric Wilson, the loss prevention agent for that store, noticed the customer crawling on the floor, and asked how he could help. After she explained the situation to him, Eric got down on his hands and knees and joined the search. No luck. He took Mrs. Shaw's contact information and told her he would follow up.

Eric then contacted two employees in building services, Bart Garcia and Tom Fraley, who joined in the search. Again, no luck. Perhaps the diamond was in one of the vacuum cleaner bags? They gathered the vacuum bags, and began splitting them open and sifting through their dirty contents. Eventually, voilà! They found the 2.8-carat stone.

When Eric called Mrs. Shaw with the good news, she was thrilled to the point of tears. Soon after, her sister blogged about the experience, and others tweeted their appreciation for the team's service.

Eric Wilson took the initiative. His job description did not include scrutinizing full vacuum cleaner bags. He could have told building services about the lost diamond and then moved on with his tasks for the day. But the customer desperately wanted to find her diamond. Eric owned the situation. He figured out the best approach to solving the problem and made a difference in a person's life.

Nordstrom spread the tale throughout the company and the culture, including producing a video centered on an interview with the customer. The video clip was shown to virtually all 72,000-plus Nordstrom employees, who were encouraged to "create your own version of the 'diamond story.'"

To top it off, the video was played at the company's annual shareholders meeting in Seattle. After the clip, Erik Nordstrom told the audience, this story of customer service "raises the bar." Then he introduced Eric Wilson, Bart Garcia, and Tom Fraley, all of whom were flown in from North Carolina, along with members of their families. They were greeted with a standing ovation.

"How can we create an environment where people like them can do great things?" asked Erik. "Eric Wilson didn't ask what his job description was in loss prevention. Job one for us is to take care of the customer. Most housekeeping people view their job as cleaning the store. That's where it stops and starts. Clearly, our housekeeping folks knew that their job was taking care of customers. Here was an opportunity to take care of a customer in a different way. All of our jobs are much broader. We all have our day-to-day job of contributing to take care of customers. But now and then we are presented with opportunities to do it in a different sense, in a broader sense. That story is a great example of what's possible when we focus on the customer."

5

Humility

We were raised selling shoes, which is a humble occupation. You're down on your hands and knees, waiting on customers, which I find an appropriate position for our level of service.

—Bruce Nordstrom

Humility is a modest view of one's own importance.

Despite their success, the Nordstroms have never had an inflated opinion of themselves. Through four generations they continue to project a public image of disarming, small-town modesty that might strike the casual observer as disingenuous. They say that there is nothing special or magical or difficult about what they do and that the system is embarrassingly simple. "We outservice, not outsmart," is a typical Nordstromism.

"Our success is simply a matter of service, selection, fair pricing, hard work, and plain luck," said Elmer. "As the owners, we felt that we should work harder than anyone else. If we didn't, our lackadaisical attitude would spread to the next level, and the next level on down until everyone was taking it easy."

In 1968, Elmer's son John N. told the *New York Times*, "We don't know anything the other guys don't know, and we don't have any secrets. All publicity does is give us a swelled head, and we can always do better. The salespeople are the real stars."

John N.'s brother Jim once conceded to the trade publication *Footwear News* that, "Many people think that we Nordstroms are secretive, because we don't talk much about ourselves. The truth is, we can't afford to boast. If we did, we might start to believe our own stories, get big heads, and stop trying."

The Nordstrom family views service as a personification of selflessness and humility. Noting that the company's roots are in the shoe business, Bruce has said that "kneeling in front of the customer is a literal and symbolic way of how we view our business because it says more than one thing. First, it obviously speaks to worshipping the customer and appreciating that that's where our living comes from. We wouldn't be here without the customer. Second, the shoe business is the dirtiest, hardest, most difficult part of the soft-goods business because you have to handle the inventory so much. In every other form of soft-goods retailing, most of the inventory is out on the floor, but in the case of footwear, you have to go get it in the backroom. You have to decipher what the customer has in her head. And then you have the size element; the foot is the most difficult part of the anatomy to fit. You've got to have the right size; you've got to have what they want and when they want it. So, there you are trying to do these things—humble, sweating, on your knees."

After more than three decades of interacting with members of three generations of the Nordstrom family, we are happy to report that this is no act. The Nordstroms are self-effacing people. But don't ever mistake humility for a lack of competitiveness and a powerful will to win. This was demonstrated in another endeavor: their majority ownership of the Seattle Seahawks of the National Football League from the team's inception in 1975 to when they sold the team in 1988.

Their participation in securing the franchise, "was a civic venture," said Mike McCormack, a member of the Professional Football Hall of Fame, who once served the Nordstroms as director of football operations for the Seahawks. "The local Seattle group needed a major player, so the Nordstrom family stepped up. They made a family decision for the good of the area."

The price tag was $16 million, which seems comically low by today's financial standards. The NFL insisted that one person had to be the majority owner, but none of the other Seattle investors had the required $8 million-plus. Lloyd Nordstrom convinced the NFL, particularly his friend, commissioner Pete Rozelle, to designate the Nordstrom family as the owner of 51 percent of the team. That was the first time a family, not an individual, was majority owner. It was a show of faith that the family would make unified decisions.

It was a good decision for the Nordstroms. "Lloyd was aware of the fact that if the league did well, it would bring Seattle along with it," Rozelle told us back in 1995. And it was a good decision for the NFL. "As a family, they were always on the same page. You are always going to have trouble with a club somewhere along the line on some issues, but we never had one single bit of a problem with the Nordstroms."

In more ways than one, the Nordstroms were unique owners in the NFL, seeking a degree of anonymity that is unheard of in a business where owners often battle their players for a share of the limelight. In fact, they didn't even want to have their names and pictures printed in the Seahawks media guide. John N. was the family member most involved with the team, and when it was later acquired from another owner by Paul Allen, cofounder of Microsoft, John N. joined the team's advisory board.

"Aside from football, Mr. John gave me the opportunity to learn the business of retail, and I've never forgotten that. He was looking out for me," said Sherman Smith, a former Seahawk running back and coach, in John N.'s book, entitled *Mr. John*. "He said, 'Let's talk about what you're going to do after you're done playing football.' He was always such a regular guy with us, and that's what I liked most about him."

Don't Be Cocky

When you discuss customer service with members of the Nordstrom family, they frequently use the word humble, which is not often heard in corporate offices and boardrooms. They believe that a commitment to service requires employees to put themselves in the shoes of the customer.

"If you are really looking to the customer, if you're really sensitive to the customer, and sensitive to the people on the front line, you are aware of your shortcomings," said Erik. "That keeps us focused on the things that are necessary in order to give [great] customer service."

His brother Blake added, "It's not about us." He described his role and that of his family members as "stewards of the business and the culture. We are here to help everyone achieve his or her goals. Companies that have a strong culture have an asset—a point of difference. We try to create an atmosphere where people feel valued, trusted, respected, and empowered, where they have a proprietary feeling and an entrepreneurial spirit. The magic occurs when all these things come together."

Erik said, "We like to tell stories around here. Not a day goes by when the three of us don't communicate with customers."

A retired company executive noted, "There's something magical about how the Nordstroms feel toward the customer that just connects with employees. The passion of the Nordstrom family for this business is hard to replicate. It's so powerful when they come around to talk to our people and remind them that our company is only as good as they are today and every day." That executive cited how meaningful it is for frontline people to have a Nordstrom family member visit their store and ask them what they need to do their job better. "The people on the sales floor think: If these Nordstroms are fighting it out, I'm going to fight it out, too."

What's fascinating is that Nordstrom does not boast about its service to the outside world. The company never runs advertisements crowing about its customer service, nor does it ever send out press releases blowing its own horn about the company's customer service. Top company executives rarely comment on customer service to the press. Nordstrom does not brag about its customer service because it knows it can always get better. In fact, the company goal every year is to improve its customer service. Yes, even Nordstrom believes there is always room to get better.

"Fortunately, there is no secret formula," said Blake. "Otherwise, many of our competitors would have discovered and adopted it."

As one Nordstrom executive once told us: "It's not that we're so good, it's that everyone else is so bad, and we look better by comparison. The moment we get cocky is the moment that we hand a shoe box to the customer with two left shoes. Our reputation is only as good as our last customer experience."

Adrienne Hixon, a store manager, said, "It's a daily thing. We can take two steps forward with one customer and then go 20 steps backward with the next phone call. I'm humbled every day through customer feedback."

Nevertheless, Nordstrom's reputation for customer service has spread throughout the world. We have given keynote speeches and workshops about the company in a couple of dozen countries in every part of the world. Even people in London, Mumbai, and Sydney who have never set foot in a Nordstrom store, are aware that Nordstrom is known for its service.

If Nordstrom doesn't advertise or boast about its service culture, how has the reputation spread? The answer is simple: word-of-mouth, which is the most powerful advertising of all.

"If we sell you well, tell others. If not, tell us," read a sign on the first Nordstrom store a century ago. Though the forms of "telling others" have changed, the dedication to service remains the same.

Today's customers are smarter and are armed with more knowledge that at any time in the history of commerce. Consequently, smart companies must be smarter and more knowledgeable.

"Hopefully, we have the humility to understand that our customers are better informed than ever because they have access to great product information right on their own mobile device," said chief innovation officer Geevy Thomas. "We have to be sponges. We have to be present with our customers, attentive and empathetic to their needs in the moment. We need to anticipate their needs and fulfill them before they ask."

Starting at the Bottom

Virtually all employees—including people whose last name is Nordstrom—begin their careers on the selling floor, before they rise up through the ranks to become managers. The founder's three sons all began working in the store by the time each of them reached the age of 12, establishing a Nordstrom family tradition that continues to the fourth generation, each member of which worked in the store through high school and college. At various times, all the Nordstrom family members have been buyers, merchandisers, department managers, store managers, and regional managers.

"Our family was well served by not having succession determined by votes of stock or battles within the family," said Erik. "The stockroom was open to anyone who wanted to grab a shoehorn. Most of my generation did to some degree. It was nice for us to have that latitude to explore what we wanted to do. My brothers and my cousin Jamie and I ended up liking it and sticking with it all these years. Our cousins chose to do other things. It was all very natural. There's not a lot of drama in my family."

Erik felt it was a natural progression for him and his brothers to start working in stock and then move on "to co-third assistant in women's shoes, then to a second assistant," and so on, long before ever taking on any management responsibilities. "We were all well served by that. In our culture, you learn by doing it."

His older brother Pete said, "I can't imagine doing my job, or any job I've ever had in this company, without being grounded in how it all plays out at the point of sale. For example, I would be of no help to a salesperson who has a question about returning a suit if I hadn't done that exact same thing a few times myself."

Starting on the sales floor sends the signal from management that it values that role more than almost anything. All up and down the organization, people appreciate the importance of this function and what it means for everything else in the organization.

"No matter who you are reporting to, at one point, they did what you're doing," said regional manager Greg Holland. "I've sold, I've been a buyer, a store manager, a regional manager. I can look anybody in the eye and say, "I relate to you and what you're doing. I understand. I've been there.'"

Clear evidence of this culture of upward mobility is that only a small handful of corporate officers (in specialized roles) came from outside the company; all of the others rose from the stockroom and the selling floor.

Nordstrom employees universally appreciate the promote-from-within policy because it creates a culture where every manager and every buyer has gone through the same experiences as the people he or she is managing. No one manages until he or she has "walked in the shoes" of those being managed.

You start at the bottom and do it the Nordstrom Way, and those standards are nonnegotiable.

Servant Leadership and the Inverted Pyramid

Nordstrom's Inverted Pyramid (see figure 5.1), which we talked about in Chapter 1, is not merely a symbol; it is the way that Nordstrom runs its business.

"When business gets tough, invariably that Pyramid starts to tip," says Blake. "The minute a manager starts walking around thinking, 'I'm the boss and I have all the answers,' it doesn't work. If the culture is strong enough, it bitterly rejects that."

OUR CUSTOMER
COMES FIRST

We took the traditional corporate pyramid (you know, the one with the
executives at the top) and turned it on its head. The Inverted Pyramid reminds
us that we value those working closest to our customer.

CUSTOMERS

SALES & SUPPORT PEOPLE

DEPARTMENT MANAGERS

STORE MANAGERS, REGIONAL MANAGERS,
CORPORATE HEADQUARTERS

EXECUTIVE TEAM,
BOARD OF DIRECTORS

Figure 5.1   Inverted Pyramid

To Adrienne Hixon, a store manager, "Anyone who is promoted understands that you're moving down the Pyramid, not up. You are taking on more responsibility to support the people above you. What has worked at Nordstrom is having a living, breathing understanding of servant leadership, making sure that everyone on the team knows what servant leadership is. You're not going to ask other people to do something that you're not willing to do yourself. That is a core value that's worked over the past century-plus."

Leaders in workplaces where there is a high level of trust are comfortable asking for help from colleagues, which increases their trust and cooperation. "Asking for help is effective because it taps into the natural human impulse to cooperate with others," writes professor Paul Zak.

For manager Callie Hutton, it's having an awareness that it takes a team working together to achieve their goals. "If you are taking all the accolades for yourself, it shows through and your team doesn't want to work for you. Every day I thank people for what they did yesterday, and I am telling them what I expect from them today. To get people to want to work for you, you show that you care for them as a person who helped you get to where you are today."

What Nordstrom Owes to Its Employees

"Employees are taking their character, reputation, and integrity—and deciding to associate with us," said Blake. "Can they go home at the end of the day and be proud of the company they work for and the people they work with? Are we providing them with an environment that trusts, values, hears, and respects them?

"When you come in the door and you've heard good things about Nordstrom, you find out that we're human, we make mistakes. We are trying to create a culture and an environment that allows an individual to make a difference. If you feel you're just a number punching a clock, it will not work. We need 72,000 people to feel that this is their deal. We've got to listen to them talk about how we're going to improve every day. If we can do that, we're excited about what's possible."

Nordstrom doesn't give out figures on its annual employee turnover, but the company will say that although its turnover rate is lower than other retailers, it can always improve.

"We have lots of opportunities," said Blake. "We work hard to attract somebody to be on our team. We want to do a good job of listening, and to give them the tools to be able to reach and exceed their goals. If someone stays two years with us, they tend to stick.

After two years, our turnover goes down considerably. The majority of leaders began their careers on the sales floor. More than 26,000 employees have been with Nordstrom from 2 to 11 years."

It's not uncommon for people who started on the sales floor or in the stockroom to stay with the company for 20 years or more, taking on new assignments as they grow.

The Rack offers a first-time employment opportunity and a developing ground in which department managers, store managers, and people in other key positions can grow as leaders. One general merchandise manager said, "The number one thing I learned at the Rack is that the best ideas come from the floor. That's something I practice to this day as I get out in the stores and listen to our people. It makes a big difference in your business. The Rack experience reminds you of the importance of the team, and the importance of each player being the best at their position. You must surround yourself with the best people, articulate the expectations, and then let them soar."

New Markets

Because Nordstrom considers its culture the key element separating it from the competition, when the company expands to other regions, it relies on experienced Nordies to bring the culture with them and to teach and inspire new employees to provide customer service the Nordstrom Way. They are motivated by opportunities to move ahead in the company and to have the experience of being involved in building something from the ground up.

When Nordstrom expanded into Canada in 2014, the company treaded softly and humbly in order to make the best impression. When another major retailer, Target, entered Canada, it took a we-know-best approach and the results were disastrous. Target eventually retreated from Canada and was forced to take a write-off of $1 billion. Nordstrom adopted the opposite attitude.

"We don't assume anything," said Karen McKibbin, then president of Nordstrom Canada. "Earning our customers' trust isn't something we take lightly, and we're going to work hard to compete and give customers a reason to choose us. . . . We are going to stub our toe. We are not going to get everything perfect."

Instead of opening four stores within short succession, Nordstrom spaced out the openings so the company could learn from its mistakes and make "the adjustments, things that customers are telling us they want, and then apply that to our next store," said McKibbin. They made sure that they did it right because you only get one shot.

Because expanding to Canada with six new stores over a three-year period was the biggest challenge to the culture, Nordstrom changed the way it trained people. Although Nordstrom historically promotes from within, it was unable to do that in Canada because it wanted the stores to be filled with Canadian employees. For the first time in company history, Nordstrom hired people that had never been in the stores nor were familiar with the Nordstrom Way. They hired dozens of Canadian managers, who were brought to Seattle for three months to be assistant managers in each of their respective departments in the company's Bellevue store. They eventually went back to their markets, hired their crews, and brought the culture with them.

Humility

No employee at Nordstrom is above doing a little housekeeping. That includes people named Nordstrom.

A woman who had worked at Nordstrom in the 1980s told Robert Spector a story about Bruce Nordstrom walking through her department one day. Bruce spotted a can of pop on the counter. He picked up the can, deposited it in a wastebasket, and continued on his way. He didn't ask who was responsible for the can being on the counter and he didn't order an employee to take it away. He just did it himself. This woman, who went on to run several of her own successful businesses, never forgot the day that she saw the chairman of the company set an example for her—without his even uttering a word.

"If Bruce Nordstrom was not above doing a little housekeeping, then neither is anyone else," she said.

The Honest Truth

Trust builds loyalty with team members who will not be afraid to tell you bad news.

Sometimes you need to hear things from your team that are not pleasant. In the late 1990s, Nordstrom went through a difficult stretch, which culminated in the then-CEO of the company being fired and replaced by Blake of the fourth generation. Blake's father Bruce was brought out of retirement to again be chairman. Bruce and his three sons—Blake, Pete, and Erik spent the next six weeks traveling the country, speaking with top salespeople, soliciting their unvarnished opinions on what went wrong and how things could be fixed. These loyal and outstanding employees told the Nordstroms that they felt "maybe we didn't trust them anymore and we weren't listening to them, that we didn't value them as much," said Blake.

Bruce wrote in his memoir, *Leave It Better Than You Found It*, that those encounters with employees were "a tempering experience. We asked for criticism and we got it, but it was positive criticism from loyal employees. At the end, I felt strangely invigorated. These are amazing folks. They were a little ticked off and certainly had things to say. I felt so good about the amount of input I got. Listening to our people helped this company more than anything else we could have done. Ask your top people what they need, because they have the answers."

Accessibility

Within the company and the consuming public, the Nordstroms are approachable and accessible. All of the Nordstrom family and top executives are constantly visiting Nordstrom stores all over North America. "Blake Nordstrom could never be on the television program *Undercover Boss* because everyone would recognize him," joked chief innovation officer Geevy Thomas. "All of us are always in the stores. We are on the floor all the time."

Departments are trained to answer the phone on no more than the second ring. When you call a Nordstrom store, an actual person answers the phone. There is no recording offering the caller options from a menu.

All of the Nordstroms answer their own phones—and return calls. This has been true through four generations.

Jim, of the third generation, told us in the 1990s, "If I'm a supportive manager, who am I to have someone screen the calls of the people who are slugging it out every day on the sales floor and doing the work? If I don't call our people back, they'll never call me again. And if they don't call me, I don't learn anything and I don't get any better."

Jim noted that when retailers from other countries would come to Seattle to study Nordstrom, they would amass "a big stack of notes. When I asked them what they were going to do with all their notes, they'd say that they were going to have sales contests and other things that we do. I asked them if they were going to answer their own phone. They said, 'No, I can't do that.' I told them, 'Then you may as well throw all those notes in the wastebasket, because it's all got to start with you.'"

Here is a pair of "like-father-like-son" stories:

"I've taken thousands of calls over the years from customers who had one thing or another to say about how we were doing our business," said Bruce.

One day, while Bruce was sitting in his office, his phone rang. Bruce picked it up and said, "Hello." After a second or two of silence, the voice on the other end asked, "Is this Bruce Nordstrom?"

Bruce said, "Yes."

After introducing himself, the man explained that he was on a break from a seminar in Toronto with the management guru Tom Peters, coauthor of *In Search of Excellence*. Before the break, Peters had told his audience that the only executive he knew who answered his own phone was Bruce Nordstrom. When the seminar went back in session after the break, Peters took the stage. Before he could get started, a man in the audience waved his hand to be called on. It was the man who had called Bruce. He told everyone what he had just experienced. Big round of applause. Peters later sent Bruce a thank-you note for validating what he had said.

When we told that story to a convention of dentists, one dentist said, "I don't answer the phone in my practice. If my staff is busy, I'll let the call go to voice mail. But, if Bruce Nordstrom isn't above answering his phone, I guess I'm not above it, either."

Bruce's son Blake estimates that he gets 20 to 30 customer calls and 20 to 30 e-mails a day, plus letters.

Seattle resident Sarah Busch, then 79 years old, opened her monthly Nordstrom statement and was disappointed that the company had changed the format she had gotten used to over many decades. She phoned Nordstrom's corporate headquarters and asked to speak to someone in management. After a few rings, a voice answered the phone.

"First of all, I'd like to know to whom I'm speaking," said Sarah Busch.

"This is Blake Nordstrom."

"Blake Nordstrom? You're the president!" a confounded Sarah Busch exclaimed.

"I am indeed."

"What are *you* doing answering the phone?"

"Well," Blake deadpanned, "I was sitting here at my desk, and the phone rang, so I picked it up."

She told Blake that she had been a loyal customer since Nordstrom was a shoe store and that she still had the first credit card Nordstrom issued when the company merged with Best Apparel in 1963 to become (temporarily) Nordstrom Best. She kept the card as a memento. But she didn't like the format of the new monthly statement.

Two days later, she received a letter from Blake, which included a brand new replica of her old Nordstrom Best credit card. They've been friends ever since.

Next time you're sitting at your desk and your phone rings, please answer it. The party on the line could be one of your most loyal customers.

6

Communication and Collaboration

Our culture lives and breathes when we have communication flowing back and forth.

—Blake Nordstrom

Communication is the imparting or exchanging of information or news; a means of connection between people or places.

There is no communication without collaboration and vice versa. You can't have teamwork without communication. You can't have communication without teamwork. And without teamwork and communication you can't inspire and empower employees to take ownership.

The essence of communication and collaboration is the forthright exchange of information, ideas, opinions, disagreements, changes, and news (both good and bad). The results are a meaningful partnership based on shared goals and win-win outcomes.

Research has shown that when employees don't feel well informed on their organization's goals and strategies, they experience increased stress, which weakens teamwork. That's a prime reason why daily communication is essential.

No matter what kind of domestic or international organization we've consulted with, virtually all of them admit that their biggest issue is communication. Any time there is more than one person involved, you have a communication challenge. Without clarity, respect, and trust, communication is impossible. Productive collaboration is a challenge because meaningful communication is so rare.

Is communication an issue in your business?

Today, with all the communication instruments at our disposal we now have more ways to miscommunicate. Emojis can be bewildering.

When was the last time you misinterpreted an emoji? Have you ever puzzled over a misspelled text message? Never assume a meaning. What if you're wrong? It's better to overcommunicate than undercommunicate.

At Nordstrom, communication begins before the store opens with the daily morning team meeting. The store manager conducts morning announcements either in person or over the intercom system so that everyone can hear the information while they prepare their departments for the day's business. The store manager provides a review of the prior day's business, highlights individuals who exemplified outstanding service, recognizes employees who had great results (such as the top 10 individual selling performances), reads customer service letters, discusses new product in the stores, gives an update on store events, and motivates employees for the day by establishing sales goals.

Sometimes, these morning announcements morph into rallies, when everyone in the store gathers together in a particular location to have face-to-face meetings and conversations on a variety of topics, such as building customer relationships, details on new merchandise, or an upcoming event such as the Anniversary Sale, held in July, which is the largest volume-driving event of the year.

"Keep it simple and make sure everyone is on the same page," said store manager Adrienne Hixon. "We talk about yesterday's results, the priority of the day, what's happening in the store and the things we want to work on. We recognize birthdays, years of service, and the fun things that make this an enjoyable place to work. We are all part of a team. If the team doesn't work, the dream doesn't work."

Communicate, Communicate, Communicate

The company communicates with all 72,000-plus employees in a variety of directions and channels—corporately, regionally, locally, within stores, within divisions, within departments, and so on, using e-mail, company intranet, blogs, and other technology including the good old telephone. Nordstrom uses all these touchpoints in order to maintain and enhance the culture, to get alignment, and to get feedback on strengths and opportunities to improve.

Leaders must be in close contact with their teams to avoid uncertainty and misinterpretation. At Nordstrom, whenever there is an announcement of a major change in the business or an important new initiative, the company's strategy is for the information to "trickle up" the Inverted Pyramid in face-to-face meetings.

Regional managers are responsible for communicating information to their store manager teams; store managers are responsible for relaying the messages to their department manager teams; department managers are responsible for passing the information on to those at the front lines. The simple idea is to keep everyone abreast of what's going on.

Employees receive e-mailed articles on the shared culture and common purpose of driving results and improving customer service, as well as general company news, philanthropic efforts, customer service letters, fashion trends, selling-related features, and company-wide employee recognition.

Letters of complaint about customer service (omitting the names of the offending salespeople) are also read over the store intercom.

Nordstrom sends out monthly and quarterly e-mails announcing sales results, recognizing individual and team achievement, and alerting people to upcoming special events and new initiatives.

At the annual State of the Company employee meetings, management talks about past results and future goals, the game plan for the new year, how profits are divided, and so on.

Using internal "connect boards," employees can anonymously submit questions, suggestions, or concerns. Usually within 24 hours, the appropriate person or team will follow up with an answer. Through this system, store managers get to hear what's on the minds of their team members and then have the opportunity to respond. This forthright communication strengthens the connection between salespeople and support groups and builds the sense of the whole store as a team.

Nordstrom has an open-door policy, where managers and executives are always available to converse with each other by any and every means necessary. During orientation, the company tells new employees: "Our door is always open. It's important to us that every person who works here feels valued, welcome, and cared for."

Shared Leadership

Management by consensus has been a hallmark of Nordstrom. John W.'s three sons—Everett, Elmer, and Lloyd shared the leadership during their tenure. The brothers realized that their ability to work well together was crucial to the success of the business. Their relationship was akin to a marriage. "You worked together for a common goal, but you didn't get your own way all the time," said Elmer. Options were weighed and discussed as a team. Disagreements were resolved by majority rule.

When they retired, their sons Bruce, John N., Jim, and Lloyd's son-in-law Jack MacMillan applied those lessons to their own leadership of the company.

"Our dads set a great example for us," Bruce wrote in his memoir. "They'd go into a meeting, shut the door, and always came out of that meeting of one mind. That's what we wanted to do. To understand the dynamics of our committee, you have to know that we started with the unanimous feeling that we wanted to be of one mind—not that we didn't want to disagree with one another, because that was the strength of our setup. We all had the same goal, but we had different thoughts on how to reach that goal. To me, if you've got the right people, you'll come out with the right answer more often than not."

That approach was emulated by the fourth generation, Bruce's sons Blake, Pete, and Erik.

"My brothers and I never decide an issue by a vote," said Erik. "What means more is the strength of someone's convictions. You may be the one who has a different view than the other two. Your choice is either to convince the other two by the strength of your convictions or agree with them. We do the same with our executive team. It's not about people's titles or how many votes someone has. If you disagree, then you have a responsibility to present your view. If it's a good argument, it's going to carry the day. We are better as a team than we are individually. That has to guide your behavior."

Face-to-Face Communication

Even with all the electronic channels of communication, Nordstrom believes that there's no better channel than in-person, face-to-face. The company conducts periodic, regional town hall meetings where employees have personal interaction with members of the Nordstrom family and other officers and managers.

"Listening to everyone is important," said Blake. "It's good having a big family. There's lots of us. My brothers and I and our executive team spend over half of our time on the road—an average of three days a week. We meet with every employee. It takes us a month. We are out there trying to kick tires and stay close to the business and take that back to what we're doing."

Nader Shafii, a million-dollar salesman in the South Coast Plaza store in Costa Mesa, California, recalled early in his career the opportunity to encounter members of the Nordstrom family at store meetings, where they would walk around the store and talk to the people on the floor.

"As a business graduate, I was impressed that the copresidents of the company would talk to the sales staff on the floor and ask questions," said Shafii. "It intrigued me. I felt the warmth, the closeness among the managers and staff. You did not feel it was a boss/subordinate relationship. That's when I started to look more seriously at a career in retail. The more I listened to them speak, the more I understood what this company is based on. It changed me from wanting to have a job to having a career. I stayed in retail, specifically at Nordstrom, because of who these people were."

Greg Holland, a regional manager, said: "We can't communicate enough with our employees. Every quarter I ask, 'How can I, as a servant leader, help you achieve the objectives that we've agreed upon?' I ask managers to share the three things that they are: (1) most proud of; (2) would like to do differently; and (3) going to achieve this year. We communicate and collaborate on how we're going to get all that nailed [down]."

Communication with the sales staff is obviously an essential part of the buyer's job. Nordstrom's best buyers support the salespeople in the stores. The buyers work for the salespeople; the salespeople don't work for the buyers. That's what Nordstrom's Inverted Pyramid structure is all about.

"My customer service is to my managers and salespeople because they are talking to the customers," says a buyer. "I need their feedback to help shape my buy."

Buyers get their feedback directly from the salespeople and the customers because they are encouraged to spend several hours a week on the sales floor. Interacting with the customer is powerful. Computer spreadsheets can tell you what's selling, but they can't tell you what you're not selling because you don't have it in stock. The best buyers at Nordstrom are good listeners. Customers appreciate being able to talk directly with a manager or a buyer. If a customer wants to know when a particular shoe will be in stock, a salesperson can turn to his or her buyer or manager and get the answer immediately.

Nordstrom has many ways to get feedback from the people on the sales floor. For example, every year, the company flies in to Seattle all the salespeople who have recorded a million dollars or more in sales.

"We are closest to the market," said Van Mensah, a million-dollar performer. "We talk about different trends, what we need to do to improve the business. A lot of the things we talk about get implemented. We give that advice freely. The company saves a lot of money by getting advice from people inside the company rather than bringing in a consultant who has no clue on how to sell to a customer. Our markets are different. By bringing in all these people from different markets, you get a good idea of your total business."

Salespeople are asked to provide immediate feedback to the department manager on the quality, construction, fit, and availability of every product they sell so that the manager can respond accordingly.

At the Rack, Nordstrom's clearance store division, they send out informal surveys to employees, called "What Would You Do?" to get insight into topics such as improving service and "What two things can we improve upon in your department and/or store?"

Because salespeople are so close to the customer, their feedback is essential for upper management. Nordstrom management finds ways—official and unofficial—for salespeople to advise on topics such as floor layout and design.

Nader Shafii recollected a meeting where then-cochairman Jim Nordstrom (who died in 1996) addressed buyers and managers and some Pacesetters, who are the highest achieving salespeople in their respective departments.

"Mr. Jim told the buyers and managers that the salespeople on the floor were the most important people in the company because they are the people between management and the customers," recalled Shafii.

"He said, 'The salespeople are the ones who can bring the message from the customers to management—they tell us what they need in order to be able to make the customers happy. If the salespeople are not happy with the product, the buyers and managers should know. You should be able to react to that.' That was a huge statement. That was the turning point for me."

When we once asked Jim about the importance of listening he said, "The person we are going to learn from is the one who's actually doing the work. The guy I'm willing to trust is the guy who knows how our loading dock should be laid out, and when we should open it up and when we should close it. That guy understands how to make things better."

The department managers are the shopkeepers, accountable for hiring and coaching. They need to be on the floor, rubbing elbows, coaching in the moment.

"Communication up and down the Pyramid is essential," said manager Nancy Love. "Patience, creativity, persuasion, and respect for all aspects of the business. These experiences made me a better store manager because I understood the dynamics of making changes to our merchandise mix and what it took to make those changes happen."

It's imperative for your organization to regularly ask your frontline people their thoughts on how they can do their job better. Start out with this simple question: "How can I make your life easier?" We guarantee that they will have plenty of answers—and most of the time those ideas won't cost you any extra money. Try it.

Hearing and Listening

Larry King, the U.S. television talk show host, once said, "I've never learned anything while I was talking."

Cultivate a culture of listening—to colleagues, patients, vendors, and your community. Listening is the apparatus for communication and collaboration. A good coworker is a good listener.

Nordstrom reminds its employees to, "Always be doing at least as much listening and responding as you do talking."

Most of us are hearing but not listening to what the other person is saying. Rather, we are waiting for the other person to take a breath or stop talking so we have a chance to express our brilliant thoughts.

When he started with Nordstrom in the early 1970s, Brian Tatsumura, a now-retired store manager, took note of the best salesperson in his department, Mr. Kato, and invited him to lunch. Mr. Kato said, "Anyone can talk but how do you listen, Brian? You need to listen with all of your senses." That simple question changed his approach with each and every customer.

David Witman, another retired executive, said, the best advice he was given throughout his career was, "Listen. You'd be surprised how much you learn if you just listen when you're surrounded by smart people."

Collaboration: Teamwork

"If you're not a team player, you won't have a long career at Nordstrom," said Bruce.

Nordstrom demands individual achievement and unselfish team-work, both of which are essential to (a) the culture, (b) the experience, and (c) the bottom line.

Teamwork may be the more important of the two. You can be a top salesperson, but you won't last if you don't also give service to your fellow employees. Nordstrom employees must be team players who make a contribution to the success of their department, store, region, and the company, particularly in team selling competitions and contests, which are essential motivating tools for the Nordstrom Way.

Nordstrom constantly reinforces the idea that when the company is at its best, it is the result of a group effort. Nordstrom is both a collection of individuals and a seamless team, with each member of that team expected to be ready, willing, and able to take care of the other members while, at the same time, taking care of the customer. Consequently, Nordstrom employees are encouraged to cherish shared experiences, celebrate achievements (both individually and collectively), and appreciate one another as part of the collaborative effort.

Here's one example: On one Saturday afternoon, a Nordstrom salesperson named Linda took a phone call from a woman who wanted to buy an outfit for a wedding that she and husband were going to attend. Her husband needed to be fitted for a suit. She told Linda that her husband had recently become partially disabled and was in a wheelchair. Linda recalled:

> When the couple arrived, all of the sizes I had pulled for the husband were wrong because his disabilities were more extensive than I had understood. Not certain how to handle the situation, I called Bob [a top menswear salesperson] and he immediately came up with someone from the tailor shop. He knew how to fit the customer's very narrow shoulders while still making the trousers work.
>
> Bob spoke with the gentleman and understood his challenges. He made him comfortable and sold him two suits with all the accessories. The wife bought her outfit from me. The best part was Bob's dedication to making sure everything was right for the couple. The wife had tears of joy in her eyes when they left.

Do you have stories like that? If you do, communicate and share them with all of your colleagues. That's how you create a collaborative culture built around your values.

These anecdotes reinforce the list of values that comprise this book and provide guidelines and inspiration for how individual team members can advance themselves as individuals. At the same time, they enhance the company's reputation, which ultimately benefits everyone.

Teamwork takes many forms at Nordstrom. Sometimes it's subtle, other times it's obvious.

On her wedding day, a customer had forgotten to pack a few items and her maid of honor had yet to buy her dress. The two women had rushed to take the hotel shuttle to the mall and had about an hour before they would have to return in order to get to the church on time.

The bride and maid of honor were greeted by a salesperson (whom we'll call Lynn) in the Mall of America store in Bloomington, Minnesota, who was apprised of the situation and the time constraints involved. Lynn picked out the perfect dress for the maid of honor, and then handed off the soon-to-be-bride and her maid of honor to a shoe salesperson.

While the two customers were trying on shoes, the original salesperson brought over earrings to complement the dress. They purchased two pairs of earrings. Putting the proverbial cherry on top of the cake, Lynn asked the store concierge to find the name and location of a mall merchant from whom the customers could buy silk flowers. That is what teamwork looks like.

Of course, the two salespeople in this story both earned commission money on those sales. But sometimes the most impressive examples of teamwork occur when salespeople don't earn a commission, when they selflessly go out of their way for the greater good of their department or their store or their region or their company—or just because it makes them feel good. This is a perfect example of the company's striving to strike a balance of customer service, teamwork, and individual achievement.

One more teamwork story:

Britton Colquitt, punter for the 2015 Super Bowl-winning Denver Broncos, and his teammates were flying to Washington, D.C., for a meeting at the White House with President Obama. Colquitt remembered that he neglected to pack the pants to his suit. His brother, Dustin, a punter for the Kansas City Chiefs, is a good friend and long-time customer of Jacob Hershewe, department manager at the Nordstrom store in Oak Park Mall in Overland Park, Kansas. Hershewe identified a pair of pants to perfectly match Colquitt's suit and connected with the punter's own stylist to get his exact measurements for tailoring. The style and size of the pants that Colquitt needed were in stock at a Nordstrom store in Washington, D.C. Amy Conway, the store manager in D.C., drove the pants to the hotel where Colquitt was staying. He needed the pants within an hour of landing, and she delivered them with 10 minutes to spare.

"I actually thought to myself, 'Here I am, a die-hard Kansas City Chiefs fan, and I'm helping out a division rival Denver Broncos player!'" Hershewe said. "I felt proud to work for a company that could provide such fantastic service, starting at one store and finishing at another across the country. We really demonstrated our 'One Nordstrom' mentality and I'm so glad we were able to make it happen, all in under an hour."

Social Media: Communicating with Customers

Social media helps drive Nordstrom's business because the company and individuals create content for people to share and comment on, as a way of building and strengthening relationships.

A Pacesetter on the East Coast views selling as the outcome of her primary focus, which is communicating. "I don't think you can be successful at Nordstrom unless you have a reason to communicate with the customer other than, 'I have something to sell you.' I like to spend a lot of time in the fitting room, asking questions, learning about the customer's life and sharing stories. Of course, I also keep them up to date on what's happening in the store and what items they might be interested in."

Top salesperson Chris Sharma says it's all about "being proactive: You have to follow up with every single transaction to make sure that customers are happy with alterations, how they like the product, the style. I check new merchandise every single day and stay in touch with customers."

Sharma uses all of his tools to communicate with his customers in order to create business for himself. When he first started with the company in the early 1990s, he communicated with a handwritten thank-you note after every sale. Communication then evolved to phone calls, then e-mails, then text messaging.

In that spirit, Nordstrom encourages salespeople to communicate with their customers via e-mail, text messages, Twitter, or Facebook and make comments in other forums such as Yelp. Nordstrom tells its employees: "Whichever approach your customer prefers, that's the best way to do it."

Using the website and customer input and feedback from its Facebook page and Twitter stream, Nordstrom fine-tunes offerings, from both a story and a product standpoint. Nordstrom passes those customer comments on to the people responsible for making decisions and responding to the customer.

Salespeople send out messages and photos to their followers to let them know about exclusive items in the store or upcoming events, and they share their expertise, advice, and recommendations.

Nordstrom takes a leap of faith in empowering employees to represent the company in a sales capacity. "Use good judgment"—Nordstrom's one rule—still applies to the use of social media, without restricting what employees should say or do. Nordstrom suggests some topics to avoid, but it encourages employees to have fun and to build on their relationships with customers and each other. Social media guidelines are shared with all employees who participate and are posted for the public to view at the company website.

Nordstrom expects employees to be positive, respectful, considerate, and inclusive; to always treat others (including customers, noncustomers, shareholders, coworkers, vendors, and competitors) as they would expect to be treated. Although they are approved to represent Nordstrom, they must state that the views they express in their postings and other communications are their own. They are asked not to publish, post, or release information that is considered confidential or not meant for the public, such as strategies and forecasts; legal issues or future promotions and activities; merchandise pricing information or comparisons; nor should they give out private and personal information.

This being Nordstrom, employees are expected to be humble.

"Stay away from boasting about customer service," the company tells its employees involved in social networking. "Let's stay focused on working to deliver great service instead of talking about it."

A personal stylist in Florida helps her customers do most of their shopping via e-mail and texts. "I can connect with them quickly and be more accessible. Before our Anniversary Sale, I edit down the choices appropriate for each customer, and then send small-resolution images that I get from nordstrom.com or photos I take myself. Instead of spending 20 minutes on the phone trying to describe an item to a customer, it's right there in front of them on their computer or phone."

A Seattle women's wear salesperson periodically takes pictures of items she thinks her customers would like and sends them via e-mail, text, Facebook, Twitter, and Tumblr. One of her customers wrote:

I always buy because she knows exactly what I have in my closet and what I need. Not just clothes, but also jewelry, shoes, cosmetics, and hosiery. When I tell her where I am going for a business trip and what the weather is going to be, she sends me what I don't have and then e-mails a list of my outfits for the day. This is *a dream* for a busy businessperson and mom like me.

Although she moved from New Jersey to Long Island, New York, a customer named Molly still shops at the Nordstrom in New Jersey's Garden State Plaza because of the communication she has with Keith Charles, a personal stylist, whom Molly describes as "very educated about every single thing. There's a lot of energy around Keith."

To which Keith replied, "My customers are confident that whatever I put together is a home run. I want my customers to think 'Keith is the guy who's going to make it happen.' That's what I live for."

7

Competition and Compensation

In our system, employees must have a competitive spirit because we start comparing them the day they walk in the door. That's one of the best ways we know how to improve. If we have competitive people, we can accomplish something.

—James F. Nordstrom

7

Competition and Compensation

Competition means striving to gain or win something by defeating or establishing superiority over others who are trying to do the same.

Like competitive athletes, Nordstrom salespeople are motivated in a variety of ways to give extraordinary service because great service produces extraordinary sales volumes.

Nurturing goes only so far. Monetary compensation must be part of the equation. Nordstrom believes in paying people according to their achievements, to put them in a position to be able to earn as much as their talents and efforts can generate.

The company has survived and thrived since 1901 because of its culture of service that attracts competitive goal-oriented people and treats them with respect and rewards them for their hard work and results—both as individuals and as members of teams—store, individual departments, product categories, and regions within the company. Nordstrom has always emphasized service because the better the service the better the sales, and the more loyal the customers.

"The single most important reason we try to provide great service is this: It enables us to sell more," said Blake. "The best way for our company to achieve results is to do what's best for the customer."

While that may sound simple, it's easier said than done. It's inevitable that most companies and individuals get caught up in the day-to-day activities and do not focus on outcomes.

Is customer service quantifiable? People often ask what kind of metrics Nordstrom uses to measure the effectiveness of its customer service strategy. The answer: "Are sales up or down?" Customers vote with their hard-earned dollars. As they say at Nordstrom, "Sales are the truth."

Employees are evaluated through performance metrics, by what they bring to the bottom line, not who they know.

Nordstrom is about selling. You don't rack up more than 15 billion dollars in annual sales by just smiling and being nice.

New hires are told that they can make as much money as they want to make. Nordstrom doesn't put a cap on their earning potential. The company gives them all the tools they need, so all they have to do is sell.

It's important to have veteran salespeople, particularly Pacesetters, on the floor with new salespeople so that they can learn from each other. A young salesperson could teach a veteran how to use social media and texting tools to communicate and sell.

Everett, Elmer, and Lloyd, who bought the business from their father, John W., in the late 1920s, knew that the best way to attract and retain motivated self-starters was to create a sales-driven entrepreneurial culture, and to pay their salespeople according to their ability, as we saw in Chapter 2. They did it as a matter of survival.

"We were all a bit retiring and weren't particularly strong salesmen," Elmer wrote in *A Winning Team*, the privately published family history. "In fact, others could sell rings around us."

Aware of their own selling limitations, they hired people who could move the product. In so doing, they established a culture where outstanding employees would be rewarded for achieving sales goals. They recruited "fiery producers, tough guys, men who had to work hard to put bread on the table," Elmer said. Hiring these self-described "shoe dogs," who were attracted to the Nordstrom system where employees earned commissions on each and every shoe sale, "was usually a shot in the dark. In most cases, we just looked them over, gave them a shoe horn, and watched how they performed."

That philosophy still holds true today. A college degree is not important at Nordstrom because it can't replace a can-do attitude, a positive personality, and a strong work ethic.

All Nordstrom salespeople are paid an hourly wage, but where they make their real money—and their long-term careers—is on the commission they make on everything they sell. Commission sales and bonuses give them added incentive to work harder, and by working harder, they are able to build a loyal customer following.

To motivate salespeople and managers, Nordstrom constantly runs sales contests. From their earliest days, the Nordstroms (all of whom are intensely interested in sports and are big boosters of the University of Washington's athletic department) initiated sales competitions to promote rivalry among salespeople. If the store was overstocked in red pumps, for example, they would have a red-pump-selling contest, with the top sales performers rewarded with cash, flowers, dinners, or trips. "In a sense, every day was a contest," Elmer recalled. "Everyone tried to do their best, so that they wouldn't be stuck at the bottom of the list."

To this day, all managers know how their peers are doing. They see the numbers. It's common for department managers and store managers to create a network and learn from each other. For example, if one store is doing well selling a particular item, that manager will tell the others how they did it. The friendly competition makes everybody work harder. It lights a fire.

"Every employee's performance is their resume," said Blake. "Everything we do is performance-related. We are constantly looking at the numbers and competing. We are all frustrated athletes. It's fun to be in this business because there are opportunities every day."

Nordstrom is not just another department store. Many people think of a department store as a place where you hang out for a while before you get a real job. At most other department stores, employees are clerks—powerless functionaries, who slavishly follow the rules, don't make waves, and aren't motivated to give good service. At Nordstrom, the worst thing you can say about a salesperson is that he or she is just "clerking" it.

Nordstrom's top sales performers wouldn't change the commission-oriented, goal-oriented system because competition—both external and internal—stokes their competitive fires. That wouldn't happen if they were paid only an hourly rate. Knowing that their commission reflects how hard they work instills a different kind of drive, based on what they produce.

Nordstrom is looking to hire entrepreneurs—empowered self-starters, who seize opportunities to create and build their own businesses, to be franchisees within the larger Nordstrom franchise. To help them take ownership of their business and to build it up into a thriving enterprise, the company gives them the necessary tools, such as inviting stores, ample merchandise, state of the art inventory and replenishment systems, electronic tools to do business in today's retail world, and thank-you notes.

Nordstrom management is keenly aware that every employee will eventually have an impact on the customer experience—whether they're on the front lines or in a support position. Because the company empowers employees to treat the business as if it were their own, it seeks entrepreneurs who create excitement and passion around their business, and who can also build strong relationships, both with the customer and with other team members throughout the entire company. In the words of Niccolo Machiavelli, the Italian author and historian of the fifteenth century, "Entrepreneurs are simply those who understand that there is little difference between obstacle and opportunity and are able to turn both to their advantage."

New employees are put out on the sales floor and expected to grasp the values and expectations of the culture. They either catch it or they don't. They have to prove to management (and to themselves) that they believe in helping others and that they like to give customer service. They must have a thorough knowledge of the products and services because it is through those products and services that relationships with customers are created, nurtured, and maintained.

In the employee areas (hallways, elevators, stockrooms, and so on), reminders of selling are constant. Signs are posted that ensure that everyone understands the same philosophy of service and selling. There is a "How Much Can You Sell?" bulletin board with advice on how to improve one's results.

Commissions

Commission rewards the extra effort and it encourages the behaviors and outcomes you want. You want repeat customers. You want raving fans. You want customers to tell others that's where they should shop and that's the salesperson you should see. Commission aligns with that. Commission sales are a prime reason why Nordstrom salespeople embrace the empowerment that the company affords them. Two-thirds of employees have a variable pay component to their total compensation. That means they have the opportunity to increase their pay when they achieve results against defined targets or milestones. This philosophy of pay for performance motivates frontline people to challenge themselves and their teams to greater achievements.

The standard commission at Nordstrom is 6.75 percent on apparel sales. Commission rates vary according to product category.

Each salesperson has a designated draw, which varies with each department and is determined by dividing the hourly rate by the percentage of commission. That hourly rate varies, depending on the prevailing rate in each region. At the end of each pay period, sales-per-hour performance is calculated by taking the gross dollar volume of items sold, subtracting returns, and dividing that figure by the number of hours worked. For example, a salesperson rings up $22,000 in sales in an 80-hour pay period. Subtract $2,000 for returns, and the net total sales are $20,000, or $250 per hour. That salesperson's commission for the pay period is 6.75 percent of $20,000, or $1,350.

Top salespeople can make more than $200,000 annually. The average department manager's salary is $49,500 per year, but a manager can earn six figures depending on several factors including individual performance, sales volume, and whether the manager is opening a new store or supporting an existing store.

Like all top Nordstrom salespeople, Nader Shafii feels that he is running his own business, with the support of every level of management, and "If you are willing to go above and beyond the call of duty, Nordstrom is 100 percent behind you. You have all the support and all the tools. It's up to you to see where you would like to go with it."

If salespeople fail to make enough in commissions to cover their draw, Nordstrom makes up the difference between commissions earned and their hourly rate. Employees who fail to regularly exceed their draw get special coaching by their department manager. If it doesn't appear that a career in sales is for them, they are either assigned to a nonsales area or are let go.

One of the most important performance barometers is sales-per-hour, or SPH, in the Nordstrom mother tongue. Each employee's semimonthly sales-per-hour figures are posted clearly in a back room of the store for everyone in the department to see. Therefore, you know how I'm doing and I know how you're doing. Needless to say, the bottom of the standings is not where you want to be.

Nordstrom's nonstop emphasis on sales creates a dynamic tension among employees, all of whom have ready access to sales figures from all departments and stores in the Nordstrom chain; they can compare their performance with that of their colleagues throughout the country. Every top salesperson in each store is recognized by performance rankings that reflect the previous day's sales, the number of newly opened credit accounts, or how the store performed on a company-wide initiative. There is constant benchmarking, recognizing exceptional results, and sharing useful information to help employees produce. Bulletin boards have photos of top performers, laudatory customer service letters, and stories of legendary customer service.

When individuals and departments have a successful day or are on target to meet their sales goals, they are praised over the store intercom during the morning announcements before the store opens. The company announces group and individual awards for categories such as outstanding sales-per-hour and sales-per-month performances.

"We look for competitiveness," said executive Greg Holland. "We want nice people who love to serve, but the frosting on the cake for the perfect applicant is to be competitive. For salespeople, we're going to give you the environment, the merchandise, the tools for you to do the job. You're a shop within a shop. Make hay and we'll pay you."

Nordstrom has always been a home for ambitious immigrants. Blake points out that a large portion of Nordstrom employees who reach sales of $1 million or more are of foreign extraction. "These people remind my dad Bruce of his grandfather [founder John W.], who came to this country with nothing and could barely speak English."

Although all of these top salespeople arrived in the United States with far greater academic credentials than John W., they do share his entrepreneurial spirit.

Van Mensah, a native of Ghana, who sells men's suits in the suburban Washington, D.C., Pentagon City, Virginia, store, is often asked to speak to new employees at Nordstrom. One of the top-performing salespeople in the chain for almost two decades, Mensah doesn't sugarcoat the demands of the job.

"Demands and expectations are high, but if you like working in an unrestricted environment, it's a great place to work," he explained. "Nordstrom provides you with great merchandise and the freedom to do what you want. I always tell people that if you're interested in retail, this is the best place to work. But you have to understand that this is not for everybody. It's a tough job, but if you have the discipline and you are willing to work hard and take the initiative, it's not that tough. After a while, it becomes easy, because you get used to so many things. It becomes a habit. With the tools and resources the company provides, there's no reason for anybody not to make it."

Top Performers

The top-performing salespeople at Nordstrom achieve the designation of Pacesetter. Pacesetter used to be determined by meeting or surpassing a pre-determined annual goal of sales volume. But, over the years, the company has tweaked the plan, to make it more easily accessible for newly hired employees and part-timers. The company now uses a sales-per-hour goal to better recognize all top-performing salespeople.

Every year, Nordstrom raises the target goal figures, depending on how many people achieved Pacesetter the year before. Generally, 8 to 12 percent of the salespeople in each division make Pacesetter. Pacesetters are given a personalized certificate of merit, business cards and note cards emblazoned with the Pacesetter designation, a 33-percent store discount credit card (13 percent more than the regular employee discount) for one year, and cash, which varies, depending upon how many years the individual has achieved Pacesetter status.

After 10 years with the company, Pacesetters receive a Nordstrom stock award, which varies depending upon how many years they have achieved Pacesetter status. Employees who achieve this status 15 or more times during their career and have at least 15 Retiree Discount years of service, regardless of their age, receive a 33 percent discount through the remainder of their employment and throughout their lifetime.

Each year, Pacesetters and other top sellers and their guests are treated to a little rest and relaxation as a thank-you for all their hard work. For example, they might be given an all-expenses-paid trip to Las Vegas or Miami Beach that includes a reception and dinner hosted by the Nordstrom family.

Becoming a Pacesetter takes dedication, hard work, and a feeling of ownership of their own business, which comes about through empowerment.

"When you have star salespeople, they ought to get paid like stars because they earn it," said Bruce.

Nordstrom compensates those who reach specific sales volume goals with additional commission, stock, and other perks. Because it's given out quarterly instead of yearly, this reward is put within reach of new salespeople. Offering newcomers an obtainable goal makes starting with Nordstrom a better initial experience.

Customer Service and Commission Selling

Some might feel that there is a dichotomy between giving spectacular customer service and earning commission sales. It's true that, in some cases, salespeople are happy to get the immediate sale and are even happier to move on to another customer. They don't see themselves in a long-term relationship with a customer because they don't see themselves in a long-term relationship with their job.

"Competition is a key element of our culture," said Blake. "If done right, a commission system encourages better service and team play."

Because they are entrepreneurial, the top Nordstrom salespeople develop, build, and nurture a clientele of regular, loyal, trusting customers who are a treasure trove of referrals. They don't look for the one spectacular sale that will make their day. Instead, they are committed to planting the seed for an ongoing business relationship and to do what's necessary to regularly nurture that seed. They would argue that, because their compensation is linked to satisfying the customer, it's in their best interest to act responsibly. The best Nordstrom salespeople know that if they take care of the customer, the dollars will follow.

Salespeople can't look at the customers with dollar signs in their eyes. With Nordstrom's liberal, virtually unconditional, money-back return policy, if people aren't happy with what they've purchased, they are going to bring it right back. So, just trying to make a sale for the sake of selling something is a waste of time for both the salesperson and the customer.

"A happy customer will refer me to her friends," said a Nordstrom salesperson. "She won't do that for someone she feels doesn't have her best interests at heart."

A Customer Service All Star and personal stylist in a store in the southeastern United States said: "I try to find out everything I can about my customers and get to know their family, too. If a man doesn't like to shop, I try to get him in the fitting room with a few things, offer him a cup of coffee, then keep bringing him stuff to try on. Meanwhile, I'm asking questions, 'Do you wear a tie to work? Do you have kids? What kind of hobbies do you have?' When the customer leaves, I make notes in my personal book. So, when I follow up or they come back in, they feel like they're dealing with a friend."

"It starts with us taking care of each other," said chief innovation officer Geevy Thomas. "The only way we can deliver service to the customer is if our people take care of each other."

Trust among coworkers is essential in a commission-based culture.

"When I'm helping a customer in the fitting room, and one of my other customers needs to get rung, I trust that my coworker will ring the customer for me so I get credit for that sales. They know that I'm going to do the same for them," said a salesperson. "When you have that level of trust and respect, the customer can sense our teamwork and camaraderie on the floor. That's a huge incentive for wanting to shop here."

The best salespeople become fashion authorities. A creative salesperson's social media presence is not just about the product but also about establishing herself or himself as a social media presence with a following on platforms such as Instagram and Pinterest. The best salespeople and stylists, in essence, become their own brand, where they can spark and facilitate conversations among friends/customers about fashion.

Cross-Selling

Salespeople can depart from their departments to sell merchandise to their customers in any department throughout the store. Nordstrom believes that once a salesperson has established rapport and a relationship with a customer and has helped that customer put together the right look, the salesperson wants to make sure all of the customer's needs are met in order to complete the package. This freedom to sell throughout the store gives go-go salespeople greater opportunity for higher sales. The most driven salespeople do store walks, talk to department managers, and pick out their favorite two items on every floor—their favorite hat or favorite tee shirt.

When finishing up with a customer in their department, a salesperson who wants to do a little cross-selling might ask: "Where are you going next?"

For example, if a customer is buying a suit in the menswear department and realizes he needs some shirts and underwear, his suit salesman can sell those items to him, even though they are in a different department. That salesman could even sell his customer a sweater for his spouse or a watch for his daughter.

That's why top salespeople learn about products in other departments. Product knowledge is power. You can't develop a relationship with a customer if you don't know your product. The more you know, the better you can serve your customer.

"My business is one-stop shopping," said a salesperson. "If it's not nailed down, I'll find it for the customer. A customer once wanted a case of hangers, so I ordered them from our distribution center. Another customer wanted to buy some of our long plastic garment bags. I don't make commission on those things, but it's part of the service I provide. I sell service, not merchandise."

Other Compensation

Company literature tells employees "It's your business: Our employees have a personal, financial, and professional stake in the success of our company. You're encouraged to take ownership of your career."

The company has a generous 401(k) plan as well as profit sharing and an employee stock-purchase plan. Like everything else at Nordstrom, the profit-sharing plan has built-in financial incentives that encourage industriousness, teamwork (don't ever forget teamwork!), customer service, and expense savings. Some long-time employees retire with profit-sharing totals in the high six figures. All employees who work more than 1,000 hours per year and are still actively employed at the end of the year participate in the plan.

Because contributions are made to the plan directly from the company's net earnings, employees have an incentive to be productive and cost-conscious. (Nordstrom's shrinkage rate—losses due to employee theft—is only 1 percent of sales, which is half the industry average.) That also promotes loyalty because employees share ownership.

"If you are part of our team, you bring your integrity, character, and reputation," says Blake. "You have a vested interest in the success of this company. So, if you see that something is not right, you will speak up and make it right."

"When I worked at Nordstrom, I felt that I was one of the owners. Everything we do as employees pays us back in profit sharing," said a retiree.

With Nordstrom's parental leave benefits, eligible birth mothers can receive up to 12 weeks paid at 100 percent (with up to six weeks enhanced maternity disability pay and up to six weeks paid bonding leave). All other eligible parents (including nonbirth, adoptive, or foster parents) are able to receive up to six weeks bonding leave, paid at 100 percent.

Team Contests

Nordstrom has always used both internal and external competition to move the organization forward. The second generation of Nordstrom brothers—Everett, Elmer, and Lloyd—didn't want to merely run a shoe store; they wanted to run the biggest and the best shoe store there was, which they did. By the mid-1960s, Nordstrom was the biggest independent shoe retailer in the United States.

"We wanted to be successful," Elmer wrote in his book *A Winning Team*. "We wanted to be the best we could. There was a good spirit of competition among the three of us. Each of us merchandised our own particular areas and we all knew how each area was doing. So if one brother was doing better than the others, it was apparent to all. We had no prizes, and we didn't boast about it, but we always knew which brother was doing the best. Knowing it only made the other two try harder. In a sense, every day was a contest because in the stockroom there was a list of salesmen ranked in order of their performance.... There's a fine line between competition and cooperation, and we always watched to make sure that no one crossed that line."

Over the course of the year, individual departments, stores, and regions are recognized for outstanding sales and customer service.

Again, these awards—fueled by the performance and success of individuals—help to foster the importance of the team.

But these contests require constant vigilance because, as one might expect, Nordstrom's emphasis on generating high sales occasionally tempts a handful of employees to try to find ways of rigging the system or outmaneuvering their teammates.

Teamwork

Also honored are departments that have sold the most of that particular month's featured item. Nordstrom loves to use intercompany competition as a tool for motivating the troops.

When it comes to building positive team relationships, employees are expected to know, understand, and support team goals, and to cooperate with—and show respect for—their coworkers throughout the company.

For example, every year, the President's Cup is awarded to the full-line stores that rack up the largest increase in comparable sales over the previous year. The competition is divided into three categories, depending on the size and sales volume of the stores. The categories are named after founder John W.'s three sons: Everett, Elmer, and Lloyd. One of the Nordstroms makes an appearance in the winning store, and presents the employees with a cash prize of as much as $100,000. A President's Cup is also awarded to the new (open two to five years) stores with highest sales increases in their category.

The hoopla around winning the President's Cup is quite the scene, with a check hand-delivered by a Nordstrom brother and a marching band.

No wonder Nordstrom has more stores that generate $100 million in annual sales than any other retailer.

The Rack stores have their own competition in three categories, based on sales volume, named for Bruce, John N., and Jim of the third generation.

Each division runs monthly Make Nordstrom Special contests, where good ideas or suggestions for improving sales, systems, or other facets of the operation are rewarded with cash. The winners are honored at the Recognition Meeting. Over the course of the year, individual departments, stores, and regions are recognized for outstanding sales and customer service. Again, these awards, which are fueled by the performance and success of individuals, help to foster the importance of the team.

For nonsales personnel, Nordstrom runs White Glove Contests, which enable employees in housekeeping and maintenance to earn cash awards for keeping their stores clean and inviting to customers. A store can't win this award unless everyone who works in the store is involved.

That's how Nordstrom ensures that every employee participates in competition and compensation.

Innovation and Adaptation

Customers increasingly expect a personalized experience that merges the richness of stores with the convenience of online.

—Blake Nordstrom

Innovation is the act or process of introducing new ideas, devices, or methods. In Nordstrom's world, innovation is the value that guides the company to relentlessly seek processes and tools to better serve customers across all channels. Adaptation is the process of change by which an organism or species becomes better suited to its environment. No organization can sustain itself unless it is in a constant state of innovation and adaptation.

Most retailers view technology as the center point and are often enamored by the newest new thing. People get excited about the latest technology, but Nordstrom asks: "What problem is that technology solving for the customer?" At Nordstrom, technology is crucial to the business, but technology in and of itself is not the company's primary focus. Nordstrom believes that innovation is about solving customers' needs and enhancing every interaction the customers have with Nordstrom.

Customer Obsessed and Digitally Enabled

Innovation at Nordstrom is about being customer obsessed and digitally enabled—not the other way around. Again, technology is important, but Nordstrom wants customer obsession to drive all of its discussions.

"Customer obsession has been a thread all the way through, but how we deliver against that obsession has changed," said chief innovation officer Geevy Thomas. "The customer is at the leading edge, not the technology. We always have to ask ourselves: 'What service or experience does a customer need that they might not even know they need? How do we excite the customer? How do we honor the time and effort it takes to come to our location?'"

Nordstrom's singular focus on its customers keeps the company disciplined, yet daring, especially in difficult financial times.

Nordstrom is not the same company today that it was five years ago. It will be a different company five years from now. Nordstrom continues to be relevant by anticipating, studying, and adjusting to changes in the marketplace, which includes embracing technology in every way that has a positive impact on the customer. The Nordstrom approach is not just technology for its own sake, but technology that's inimitably intended to make it easier and more convenient for customers to shop Nordstrom and easier and more lucrative for its employees to sell more stuff.

To better serve the customers and themselves, salespeople have on either their in-store terminals or mobile point-of-sale devices a single view of all of Nordstrom's inventory in their home store, other Nordstrom stores, Nordstrom.com, and in the distribution centers. Not only does everyone share one single electronic view of the chain's entire inventory, each salesperson has direct access to all of it in order to get it quickly to the customer.

Innovation comes in many forms, not just in technology. At Nordstrom, innovation lives with that one customer and that one salesperson at that moment of truth on the sales floor. One Nordstrom salesperson might do something for a customer in a way that is unique for the customer who may have a unique issue. That's where empowerment and good judgment come in.

A Legacy of Innovation and Adaptation _____

Ever since it began in 1901 as a single shoe store in downtown Seattle, Nordstrom has always been about innovation and adaptation. Slowly and carefully, the various generations of Nordstroms broadened their selections, added stores, introduced new lines, expanded geographically, and found new ways of generating business. For example, for many decades, Nordstrom ran dozens of leased shoe departments in department stores in the western United States and Hawaii.

Back in the 1930s, the second generation (Everett, Elmer, and Lloyd) introduced some "high tech" into the store experience with the Pedoscope, a shoe-fitting fluoroscope x-ray machine. The four-foot-high metal and walnut device, in the shape of short column, had an opening where a child or adult placed their feet, and looked through a porthole for an x-ray view of their feet and shoes. Two other viewing portholes on either side enabled the parent and a salesperson to observe the child's toes being wiggled to show how much room for the toes there was inside the shoe. The bones of the feet were clearly visible, as was the outline of the shoe, including the stitching around the edges.

Bruce recalled that the fluoroscope x-ray machine was his first memory, "of being connected in some funny way to a shoe store. Endlessly fascinating. Like countless numbers of American children, I used to love to spend all afternoon, wiggling my toes in those machines." In later years, a historian wrote that fluoroscopes proved, "as attractive and exciting to little customers as free balloons and all-day suckers, and they were a terrific help in fitting shoes."

Fast-forward to today, where Nordstrom worked with a Swedish-based company called Volumental, which uses 3-D technology to measure a shopper's most accurate shoe size. The customer steps on a platform that resembles a square-shaped digital weight scale with 3-D cameras on all four corners. This produces a volumetric scan of each foot, which measures arch length, ball, and in-step. The 3-D scan is then displayed on a tablet, which helps shoe salespeople find the ideal fit.

Product Diversification

In the 1960s, Everett, Elmer, and Lloyd wanted to create opportunities for the third generation—Bruce, John N., Jim, and son-in-law Jack McMillan—so that they would stay with the company. The brothers felt that they had to either open more shoe stores outside the Pacific Northwest (which they had outgrown) or diversify into another business. Lloyd wanted to move into women's apparel for a variety of reasons, including the fact that this new offering would perfectly complement their shoe business.

In 1963, they acquired Best's Apparel, Inc., a fashionable downtown Seattle retailer, which had a second store in downtown Portland, Oregon. The company later changed its corporate name for a few years to Nordstrom Best.

Everett, Elmer, and Lloyd believed that if you could run a shoe store, you could run any business. But their entry into apparel was initially greeted with skepticism by manufacturers who "weren't very enthused to see us on buying trips," Elmer recalled, "but that only reminded us of our early days in shoes. It was like starting over in many ways, and that was exciting. No one really believed that shoe store owners could be successful in apparel. No one except us."

Many of the new women's wear buyers and managers were [and are] women. Because the Nordstroms knew that they were lacking in knowledge about the women's apparel business, "they were very anxious to identify people who demonstrated a flair for women's apparel and move them along," recalled Cynthia Paur, who began her career in 1968 doing stock work while still a college student. "There were many jobs available for women. It all depended on what career path you wanted to take, whether it was on the merchant side or the store management side. I always felt that any job I wanted was open to me."

The apparel industry's reservations about Nordstrom continued for almost a decade. The company had a difficult time securing a lot of the hot lines that they wanted to buy. But the Nordstroms pressed on. They added men's suits and sportswear in 1968. When they eventually proved themselves, they were able to get the goods they needed in order to attract the fashion-conscious baby boom generation of consumers that helped the company grow. Today, of course, virtually every apparel and footwear vendor would kill to be on display in a Nordstrom store.

What's Next?

Nordstrom management has always asked itself, "What's next?" That's how you stay relevant. Trial and error are a part of the Nordstrom DNA—knowing that some initiatives will succeed and some will fail. Nordstrom in the early 1990s experimented with home shopping as a way to expand its sales base by providing customers with more options to buy Nordstrom products. In June 1993, Nordstrom joined with Bloomingdale's in a closed-circuit home shopping show, originating from Bloomington, Minnesota's Mall of America, where both retailers have anchor stores. The one-hour Mall of America show (produced by the National Broadcasting Company's NBC Direct subsidiary) was staged in the actual stores, and goods were ordered with a toll-free telephone number. Results were underwhelming. But you'll never know if you don't try.

Around that same time, the company introduced its Direct Sales Division, which included mail order catalogs as well as experimental forays into interactive television shopping. Nordstrom later launched its own short-lived e-mail shopping service called Nordstrom Personal Touch America, which was a collaboration with a long-distance phone carrier and a software communications company. At the time in the mid-1990s, it was revolutionary for a customer to communicate with a salesperson via e-mail. Nordstrom also explored a system that would enable airline passengers to order goods from built-in computers on the aircraft. Other companies were offering interactive shopping systems via personal computers that read CD-ROM discs, which served as electronic catalogs for merchants to display items. As we wrote in the original 1995 version of *The Nordstrom Way*, "Whatever system Nordstrom ultimately uses, the personal touch of customer service has to be a part of it." That was one prediction that proved prescient.

Nordstrom has always been aware of what was going at Amazon.com, whose headquarters in high-tech savvy Seattle are within a few blocks of Nordstrom headquarters. When Amazon successfully launched its website in July of 1995, retail changed forever. Amazon proved that people would make purchases online, even when the Internet was in its most primitive stages, and customers worried whether their credit cards were secure.

"The day 1 understood that people would be shopping electronically is when I knew we needed a website," said Dan Nordstrom in our 2002 book *Anytime, Anywhere*, which predicted the importance of multichannel service. At that time, Dan was president of Nordstrom.com. "It was apparent that the Internet would become what interactive TV had wanted to be," Dan said.

Nordstrom.com debuted for the 1998 holiday shopping season. The company developed its own website in-house, at a time when most other retailers such as Walmart and Barnes & Noble were contracting with third-party companies to sell their goods online or totally separating their online and brick-and-mortar businesses. Other retailers ignored online shopping altogether. By 2000, Nordstrom.com was selected as having the best online experience, according to Forrester Research's PowerRankings. The company continues to work on improving the online experience in the spirit of being customer obsessed and digitally enabled.

Amazon has changed the perception of how the customer wants to be served. It used to be good enough for Nordstrom to have the best selection in a geographic selection. Today, because people can buy anything in the world at their computer, Nordstrom has to be very smart in its in-store selection, which will bring people in.

Nordstrom executives challenge themselves every day by asking if each initiative they make is truly customer-focused. They question whether they are doing something because they've always done it that way or because it makes life easier for the company. Is it customer-centric or Nordstrom-centric or salesperson-centric?

At our company, RSi, we are constantly challenging our consulting clients to ask themselves this one crucial question: "In whatever I do, am I enhancing the customer experience?"

Role of Stores

Stores aren't going away. People, product, and place will always drive the brick-and-mortar world, but the role of physical stores is changing. The physical store is here to stay, because it's becoming more connected, mobile-enabled, and smarter.

In most shopping experiences, the physical store—where the tactile and sensory experiences come together—is where the ultimate buying decision is made. According to software company iQmetrix, 85 percent of consumers prefer to shop at physical stores, and 90 percent were more likely to buy when helped by a knowledgeable salesperson. Another study, by IBM and the National Retail Federation, found that 67 percent of Generation Z, also known as post-millennials (born in the mid–1990s through early 2000s) generally prefer shopping in brick-and-mortar stores; another 31 percent occasionally shop in a store. Even though this generation has grown up in the digital age, most of them still want the tactile experience that can be had only in a physical store—but only if the retailer provides a compelling in-store shopping experience where shoppers can conveniently see, feel, and try out products and immediately take them home. Instant gratification.

"The way customers are choosing to shop in a more digitally connected world continues to change, and we know we need to find ways for our stores to evolve with them," Erik said. "We have a tremendous opportunity to leverage our stores in ways that will allow us to serve customers into the future better than anyone else."

"We need to think differently about how to serve the customer," said Blake. "This is why we believe the customer remains the best filter we have when it comes to every decision we make as a business."

The Physical Store Is Digitized

The physical store is not dead; it's digitized. Stores must now encompass both worlds—the sensory experience of the physical store and the personalization and convenience of online shopping. The most successful retailers seamlessly blend both.

As John Zissimos, chief creative officer at Salesforce.com, has said, "We are now in the fourth industrial revolution, a blurring of the physical and digital worlds—with customers at its center."

Nordstrom strives to digitally connect with customers, to understand their buying history and to suggest personalized offers—all in a secure environment to safeguard personal data. "Our future is going to allow us to leverage our history but not be held prisoner by it," said chief innovation officer Geevy Thomas. "How do you leverage the newest technology to make retail more relevant, more fun, more connected from a social perspective?"

Nordstrom has evolved from being a curator of products to being a curator of service and experience, supported by product. That transition requires Nordstrom to continually find ways to add value to the store experience in order to attract the customer.

When it comes to innovation and adaptation to keep the in-store experience fresh for the customer, Olivia Kim, vice president of special projects, has been a prime mover. Kim creates impermanent pop-up shops and stores within stores for a variety of reasons: to appeal to a certain customer segment, to drive traffic to particular brands, or just to show what's new. Pop-ups create unique experiences and are relatively inexpensive because the spaces are usually smaller and temporary. They give retailers flexibility to feature certain products at certain times. Another concept called "Space" sets aside an area of the store with new, cutting-edge designer brands. That space is visually distinguished from other parts of the store by using distinctive merchandising and décor.

By supporting these new designers, Nordstrom is able to both bring in new talent to its stores and also give back to the fashion industry through supporting young artists.

Many tech companies have redefined the customer experience to be the linear acquisition of a thing and to make that transaction as fast as possible. Nordstrom, on the other hand, believes that a shopping experience in a store should have social and emotional components. Nordstrom is always looking for ways to highlight the journey of the shopping experience to appeal to the customer's senses beyond a linear transaction.

Many of its stores have phone-charging stations and a "Men's Clubhouse," which features flat-screen TVs, locally brewed beer, and free one-on-one styling. You can get your leather handbag embossed at a personalization stand in the accessories area, and there's a cocktail bar and restaurant inside the store, in addition to a candy boutique from Los Angeles-based company Sugarfina. Its downtown format of stores—in Seattle, San Francisco, Chicago, Toronto, Vancouver, and New York—has a wide variety of features, including a 24-hour concierge service for late-night fashion emergencies; an extra-spacious "girlfriend" fitting room to accommodate groups of women who shop together; and a children's shoe department that hosts monthly shoe-tying classes.

In preparing for its first store in Manhattan, Jamie Nordstrom said, "We don't want to just be the best store in New York. We want to be the store [about which] somebody who travels to New York from Istanbul says, 'When I visit in New York, I've got to go see the Statue of Liberty, a Broadway show, and Nordstrom.'"

Channel Agnostic

Today's customers can shop at virtually any store, from any place, at any time, using a wide variety of tools. Customers respond favorably to retailers that are mobile, connected, convenient to shop with, and know them regardless of channel. They are empowered with product information, buying recommendations, product ratings, and price comparisons. Whether the shopping experience is in the store, online, or on the phone, customers expect a service experience that lives up to their expectations. They demand customer service that is integrated across all channels. Customers choose the channel in which they want to shop. And the retailers that do the best job of being there for them are the ones who are going to reap the rewards.

Nordstrom's leaders firmly believe that customers start with a need and then seek ways to solve that need. Customers don't think in terms of what buying channel they will use—website, store, text, or telephone—but rather what kind of experience they may desire at that moment. Consequently, Nordstrom doesn't care what channel a customer wants to use in order to buy an item. It just wants to be the customer's first choice and to serve that particular customer's needs at that moment.

One Nordstrom

Our customers love fashion and so do we. Whether they shop with us online, in our stores or both, we want to provide the best possible service experience and fashion expertise to make them feel good. Our brand is enabled by our people and built by our customers, which is why our goal is always to improve service. That's why the customer is at the center of all of our decisions.

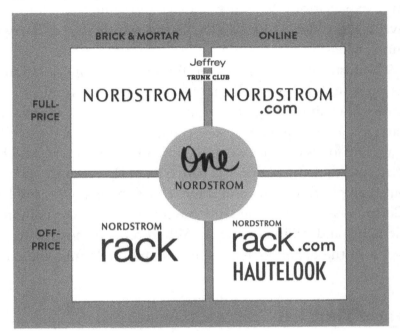

Figure 8.1   One Nordstrom

The way customers use its website influences how Nordstrom shapes its multichannel strategy, which is an important tool for acquiring—and keeping—customers. Nearly one third of Nordstrom's sales come from multichannel shoppers, who like to go online and also visit the stores. The company wants to continue to increase the number of people who shop at Nordstrom through more than one channel, because those customers spend four times as much as a one-channel shopper spends, according to the company.

When it comes to serving the end customer, Nordstrom is channel agnostic (see Figure 8.1).

"We don't have online customers or store customers. They're just customers," said Jamie. "When a customer shops with us, they don't see a difference between a Nordstrom store or Nordstrom.com. To them, it's just Nordstrom, and they want a service experience that lives up to their expectations. We work to make shopping easier for our customers by breaking down the barriers between our stores, our website, and our catalogs."

Nordstrom's focus is not on how much business it wants to do on its website, but how well the company serves its full-price customers across all channels to give customers the kinds of experiences that they can't get anywhere else.

"The focus of what we do is always the customer," said Erik. "That may sound obvious, but it is harder than that sounds. The boundaries between physical stores and Internet shopping are less and less relevant. Customers—even in the same buying journey—are combining online elements and offline elements. Wherever she shops with Nordstrom, we want the experience to be meaningful, relevant, and current."

Convenience/Time

"Customer service is not defined by us based on our legacy practices; it's defined by customers," says Pete. "Fifteen years ago, few people would define a great customer service experience as being convenient. Convenience mattered, but it was not top of mind. It was about a high-touch, person-to-person relationship. Now, it's got to be convenient and personal."

In that spirit, Nordstrom created an in-house "Convenience Center" to research how to support the retail needs of time-starved and self-directed shoppers at any touchpoint of their shopping journey. The company brings in customers and employees to the Convenience Center lab to test and provide feedback on initiatives intended to enhance personal communication between customers and salespeople.

Since 2014, Nordstrom has offered salespeople and customers the tools for their smartphones to communicate and make transactions via a secure one-to-one texting service. Customers who opt in are able to receive from a salesperson or personal stylist private text messages that contain a description or photo of one or more items. If the customer likes any of the items recommended by the salesperson, she can make the purchase by replying "buy" and using a unique code. Purchases are completed through the individual's Nordstrom.com account and are shipped directly using the retailer's free standard delivery. Text messaging enables salespeople to provide a personalized styling experience for their customers.

Customers can use their smartphone to scan any item, see the price, decide what size and color they want, and then have their purchases delivered to their home, office, or hotel anywhere in North America. Again, we're talking about convenience.

One typical scenario: A customer texts her Nordstrom salesperson that she is looking for a pair of pumps. The salesperson sends the customer a selection of pictures and descriptions of a variety of pumps. Once the customer finds the shoes that she wants to purchase, she simply taps "buy" and then gets a return text that confirms the transaction. Salespeople can earn commissions when they directly influence a customer's online purchase through an e-mail or text recommendation.

Tools like that help Nordstrom serve the customers on their terms. But what sets Nordstrom apart from many retailers is that Nordstrom uses the technology to help frontline people to better serve the customer, instead of using technology to replace frontline people.

One-third of all new Nordstrom customers come through its website. More than 25 percent of Nordstrom.com orders are fulfilled in the stores. Essentially all of the stores serve as warehouses for the online business.

Reserve & Try in Store

As we have shown, Nordstrom is constantly finding ways to make life easier for customers because customers want to shop on their own terms. Part of that strategy is to leverage its brick-and-mortar assets with e-commerce assets.

The number one question received at Nordstrom's call center is: "Can I find the item that I'm looking at online at my local Nordstrom store?'"

Because return rates are higher on online purchases, Nordstrom created Reserve & Try, which enables a customer to search and discover products online and then to quickly go to a nearby Nordstrom store to touch, feel, and try on items before buying. Reserve & Try enables customers to best utilize their own time (their most valuable resource) and helps to make the shopping experience easier.

With Reserve & Try, customers shop online and reserve items in their digital closet. Customers then fill in their contact information and confirm a reservation in the store closest to them. Users can select up to 10 things, which are held until the store closes the next day. There is no payment up front. Within two hours or less (during store hours), the store notifies customers via text message when the items can be available to be tried on. In the store, customers visit a designated department called Order Pickup for online orders and reservations. They find their name on the door of a preset fitting room, and inside are the items selected on Reserve & Try. Customers do not have to talk to a salesperson if they choose not to. They can try on the items, decide what they want to buy, and be out of the store in minutes. If customers choose to interact with a salesperson, that opens up the possibility of selling more items to them that go with their purchases.

Reserve & Try combines the convenience of online shopping with the sensory gratification of in-store shopping to create a compelling, more seamless experience across stores and online.

"The more we can focus on the customer's needs and get them done in 5 or 10 minutes—instead of 20 minutes—[the more] they're going to say, 'Hey, you gave me back 15 minutes of my life. I'll look around the store,'" said Ken Worzel, President of Nordstrom.com.

Giving the customer some unexpected extra time is a perfect example of customer obsession, which will eventually lead to good things happening.

Nordstrom also offers other time-saving conveniences such as "hems while you wait," rush alterations, drop boxes for returns, and free two-hour delivery service within a specific geographic radius. Many items can be purchased online for curbside pickup at a nearby Nordstrom store. Orders placed online are typically ready for pickup within an hour. Customers receive an e-mail letting them know when their order is ready. When arriving at the store, they call or text the number they've been given and receive delivery right in their car.

Rack

Nordstrom extends its values of adaptation and innovation to its Nordstrom Rack clearance stores, which sell Nordstrom's usual name brands at 30 to 70 percent discounts. The Rack is very efficient at selling off the odds and ends that are a natural part of the retail business. Nordstrom sends five deliveries of fresh, new merchandise a week to the Rack, which keeps bargain hunters coming back for their prey. That's a different kind of in-store experience.

The company has had the off-price concept since 1973, when the Nordstrom family opened a clearance section in the basement of the downtown Seattle store. They called the section the Rack because clearance shoes were displayed on fixtures called racks. Nordstrom initially expanded the Rack slowly and steadily, but it wasn't until after the recession of 2008 and 2009 that Nordstrom aggressively expanded this off-price business. The number of Rack stores has nearly tripled since 2010, from 86 to 215. Nordstrom expects to have 300 Nordstrom Racks by 2020.

Unlike the full-line-store customer, the Rack customer is not interested in paying full price. Nevertheless, Racks have a profound positive impact on sales at nearby full-line stores. That's why the company strategically puts Nordstrom Rack stores as close as possible to full-line Nordstrom stores—unlike other department stores that locate their clearance operations far away from their full-line stores. In downtown Seattle, Nordstrom has a Rack store directly across the street from the flagship store. The first day that Rack opened, Nordstrom's flagship had it biggest increase—pretty impressive for what was already the company's number one full-line store.

"One of the key advantages we have at Rack is our ability to leverage our relationship with the full-line stores," said chief innovation officer Geevy Thomas, who formerly ran the Rack division. "Our merchants at full-line stores have long-lasting relationships with our vendors. When a vendor has extra merchandise, Nordstrom Rack is the first place they call." This close, trusting, respectful, communicative relationship with vendors is a continuation of the Nordstrom tradition that dates back to the second generation of Everett, Elmer, and Lloyd.

Nordstrom management is very sensitive to the balance between the Rack and its full-line stores.

"We discovered from listening to customers, opening stores, and testing some different ideas, that there is a great synergy to having the Rack as part of our business," said Erik. "The Rack enhances our brand. There's a customer synergy. There are many customers who are introduced to our company through our Rack stores and introduced to the brands we carry. Forty-eight out of our top 50 vendors in our full-line stores are carried in the Rack. Although they are off-price at the Rack, there is a quality level that goes with those brands. The customers become fans of those brands, which eventually translates to the full-line stores."

A typical Rack store does approximately $500 to $550 per square foot in sales in locations approximately 35,000 square feet in size, in comparison to other off-price retailers that do approximately $200 per square foot. Several other department stores have expanded this off-price concept with mixed results.

"We execute it better than those guys," Jamie stated. "To them, it's an afterthought. It's the 5 percent of business that they never really pay much attention to. For us, it's a priority." The sweet spot for loyalty is the younger customer, whom Nordstrom first attracts through its Nordstrom Rack stores and who then become "aspirational" customers for the full-line stores. "We acquire a ton of customers through those Rack stores who migrate into full price."

Being customer obsessed and digitally enabled, Nordstrom has found—and will continue to find—ways to innovate and adapt that delight the customer and motivate employees to enhance the customer experience, create loyalty among customers, and contribute to the bottom line.

What Is the Value of a Values-Driven Culture?

Now that you are on the road to transitioning to a values-based culture, your destination is not complete until you have added the twin values of Have Fun and Give Back in your relationships with colleagues, customers, and community.

Giving back to the community can also be called "selfless service" or *seva* in Sanskrit, which is a service performed to benefit other human beings or society, without any expectation of result or award for performing it.

Nordstrom employees show up virtually every day with the desire to have fun with their customers and coworkers, because working at Nordstrom provides countless opportunities to start relationships that might last a lifetime. Of course Nordstrom employees want to make sales, but they also want to have fun, solve problems, and make someone smile.

Here's one of many examples. This is an example of how one Nordstrom employee points out the selfless service of one of her colleagues, a department manager named Jane:

> During the holidays, Jane was "Manager in Charge" for the store. She received a call to go to Santa's Chair and explain to a six-year-old girl that Santa wasn't there right now but would be back the next day. The devastated little girl told Jane that she didn't think her mom could bring her back, so she gave her wish list to Jane to personally give to Santa. Jane assured her that she would, and even gave the girl her card.
>
> The child said that if she could have only one thing, she really wanted the *Frozen* movie (and maybe a husband for her mom). This broke Jane's heart.
>
> Jane showed the list to her husband Tom and suggested they get the movie and send it to the little girl from Santa. Tom decided to buy everything on the list. The husband of Cathy, another Nordstrom employee, drives a tow truck at night, and one evening after the little girl was asleep, he and Tom arrived at her house with all the gifts on her list, as well as a tree and all the trimmings. Together, Jane and her "elves" made Christmas special for one little girl.

That's having fun and giving back.

By operating through the lens of these values, you'll want to hire only people who live these values. By doing so, you will create an environment that fosters selfless service and fun, which create a superior customer experience.

At Nordstrom, it's fun to give back and give selfless service in order to enhance our communities and our environment. Turn the page and see how they do it.

Give Back and Have Fun

Winning and success are fun and profitable, so why not devote that little extra effort?

—Everett Nordstrom

The happiest customers leave with Nordstrom bags in their hands.

—Bruce Nordstrom

In its messages to new employees, Nordstrom encourages them to have fun, adding, "Fashion is one of the truest forms of self-expression. It's creative and colorful and totally limitless. If you're passionate about fashion, this is the place for you."

As one new employee told us, "All the people who work for Nordstrom have passion about the business. You feel that they believe in what they are saying. That's inspiring. When you are sitting there listening to them, you get excited because they are so excited."

"The organization is, above all, social. It is people," wrote Peter Drucker, the management consultant. Drucker's observation is supported by the work of professor Paul J. Zak at Claremont Graduate University, who wrote in an article in *Harvard Business Review*, "When people intentionally build social ties at work, their performance improves."

A Google study found that managers who, "express interest in and concern for team members' success and personal well-being" produce higher quality performance and a greater quantity of work than managers who don't display such interest and concern. When people care about one another, they perform better because they don't want to let their teammates down.

Employee Recognition Meetings, as we discussed, in Chapter 2, are another source of fun. The upbeat meetings are intended to be entertaining and meaningful so that employees leave inspired and with a renewed sense of purpose.

The men and women who thrive at Nordstrom see fun as an essential part of their day.

Larry Smiley, a top-selling salesperson in Chicago, has the attitude that "You've got to really enjoy what you do. It's got to be a part of you. That's what makes a top seller."

Store manager Jennifer Drake said, "We see each other a lot. None of us would be putting in the time if it wasn't fun to come to work."

When you walk into a store or any business that deals with the public, you can tell almost immediately if the employees enjoy being there. At Nordstrom, you can interact with people who enjoy being there.

"Fun is the number one reason we get out of bed and do this," said store manager Adrienne Hixon. "We are here to take care of the customer. Part of that is having enthusiasm, making sure that you are enjoying what you do. If you don't enjoy it, this is a really hard job to do. We try to instill fun in everything we do, like taking inventory, or being kooky at a rally. Keeping it real is part of fun. You can see key leaders being real. Fun is essential in retail. The customer wants to have fun. We have to do it on their terms. If you're not having fun, the customer senses it and they leave."

Or as one gung-ho salesperson said, "Even on my bad days I have fun."

Does that mean we're going to have fun all the time? Of course not. Even people who create fun for a living—clowns, comedians—are not always having fun. For happy Nordstrom employees, fun is about winning internal sales competitions; making customers happy; enjoying coworkers; and being respected, trusted, and compensated accordingly. Most of us spend at least a third of our lives on the job. Let's have fun!

Fun begins in the morning in the minutes before the doors open, when the store manager gathers the team together for a quick meeting. Over the years, we have witnessed several of these meetings in Nordstrom stores all over North America. An observer can't help but note the tremendous responsibility managers have to gather up all the positivity in their being in order to pass it on to the people on the sales floor. The best managers start the day with energy, optimism, and, yes, fun. They'll single out employees who had a great day the day before. They'll read positive letters from happy customers. They'll encourage their colleagues to put forth their best efforts, as both individuals and team members—and to have fun doing it.

"It's fun to see my team make money. It's fun to see customers excited and happy. It's fun to see salespeople excited about a customer they just connected with," said store manager Jennifer Drake. "We do a lot in our culture to create an environment that's lighthearted as well as serious. Fun is important to what we do because you're more productive if the environment feels fun. We try to do things around the store to create that feeling of fun, such as store rallies and parties around things."

It's up to managers to create a fun atmosphere—within a business context.

When a long-time employee became manager of a women's apparel department at a northern California Nordstrom store, she was faced with a department that had experienced a lot of turnover.

"So my number one goal was to make sure we had stability," she said. "Once you have stability and happy people, you can create ongoing customer relationships, and that's how your business grows."

To instill a sense of ownership in her team, she divided the responsibilities in the department. She assigned each person an area of accountability, such as customer service, new accounts, and developing personal trade. The salesperson in charge of new accounts created a chart to monitor each employee's progress, encouraged her teammates, and awarded prizes to those who signed up the highest number of new accounts. The team rose to number one in new accounts for its Nordstrom store, even though it is one of the store's smallest departments. The teamwork boosted the department's spirit and, as a result, the department soon racked up the number one sales-per-hour increase in the company.

Taking this approach, "made the department more fun because each person knew they could make an impact," said the department manager. "We continually challenge each other every day to be better."

A department manager gathers her employees around her when she's coaching them and encourages them "to be a team. I'll show you how I multiple sell, how I suggestive sell. If you have two customers, turn the sitting room into a party. Let them show each other merchandise. Create a fun atmosphere. If you enjoy what you're doing, they are going to love the experience," she explained.

After all, shopping at Nordstrom is all about the experience. Fun, of course, takes lots of forms. Like finding a hot fashion item and tweeting about it to your friends. Or getting together on a shopping trip with a few girlfriends, partaking of lunch or an espresso, and taking advantage of the girlfriend dressing rooms that Nordstrom has created, where half a dozen friends can try on clothes comfortably and share their shopping experience. They might be high school girls shopping for back-to-school clothes or their moms all buying outfits for a special event. At Nordstrom, they are taken care of from head to toe—shoes, handbags, and all the accessories.

"It's everybody's job to make the customer feel good," said Jamie.

A department manager in southern California, felt that, "as long as you make the customer happy, no one has a problem with you. If you make the customer unhappy, everybody has a problem with you."

As he was winding down his career at Nordstrom, "being number one was not as important to me as it used to be," said David Butler, a now-retired, top-performing shoe salesman from the Tacoma, Washington, store. "It would have been very selfish of me not to share with other people what I was able to accomplish. I tried to help teach others what it takes to become a Pacesetter and give them the tools to do it. Helping the entire department make their day, which helped the store make its day, was a lot more fun for me."

As we've discussed, Nordstrom is a goal-oriented organization. Without goals, "you don't have a direction and you lose perspective on why you are there," said a junior sportswear buyer. "Half the challenge of the goal is making it. And when you do make it, you pat yourself on the back. And if you don't make it, you say, 'Next time, I'm going to try a little harder.'" On the other hand, "If you take a goal too seriously, it will ruin the fun of achieving it."

A saleswoman in women's shoes in the Pacific Northwest knows customers may not be able to afford everything they want each time they visit. "On the back of my business card, I write down the item the customer really wanted but didn't have time to buy or couldn't afford. I'll also enter that information in my personal book. Often, those people will come back in and say, 'Hey, I'm ready to get those boots now!' You need to develop a rapport first, so the customer has fun shopping with you."

Here's an example of a salesperson and a customer at Nordstrom's downtown San Francisco store, having fun in what could have been a stressful situation. The divorced customer, who was in the middle of making a presentation at a conference in nearby Burlingame, got a text from her college boyfriend, whom she hadn't seen in a long time. The text read: "Do you have plans tonight? Have dinner with me. Drinks at 8 at Palace Hotel. Dinner at 9."

The customer's only plans were to watch the Golden State Warriors' basketball playoff game on television. The Warriors would have to take a backseat to dinner with her college crush. As the customer wrote to Nordstrom:

> There was no way I could make it home, get glamorous, and return to San Francisco in time. How was I going to say yes to my college crush? NORDSTROM. That's how! I called the general line and asked for "personal stylist." Char Smith answered. I explained my situation, sounding a little panicked I am sure. I am 46, a single mom, and haven't been on a date in over 15 years.
>
> Char asked me questions in a calm voice about what look I was going for, did I need an entire outfit, size, etc. I said I could be there in 30 minutes, and she said she would have a dressing room ready with several options. And she did. Head to toe. Together with Eliza Abinader from TBD, we three crafted an outfit that I love: a combination of Rag & Bone, T by Alexander Wang, Dior, and Louboutin. I was date-ready and could head out of the store.
>
> Almost. I had none of my toiletries with me to freshen up. No problem. Char snuck me into the spa for a quick shower so I could rinse off my workday. She also pulled in Samantha Tryon from the spa to touch up my makeup. And once dressed, Char found my favorite perfume (Gucci Bamboo), and gave me three good doses.
>
> Char even kept me updated on the Warriors' game (though it was bad news, LOL). All the while, I was able to borrow a charger for my dying phone.
>
> And if all of this wasn't amazing enough, it got better. The finishing touch, literally and figuratively, was that Char handed me a little jar of her own styling gel. I also wear my hair in braids and needed just a little something to get the hairline smooth again. Char Smith kept this old lady on fleek.
>
> This was a wonderful experience!! I walked into Nordstrom frazzled and nervous. I walked out sleek and chic. Everyone needs this kind of glam squad. Thank you. Char is awesome. I am a customer for life.

Store Openings

Nordstrom turns fun up several notches when it opens new stores, which are huge events that are always covered by the local media. The actual opening day is completely festive. Opening day is the culmination of months of preparation by hundreds of employees, who, for the first time, are working together as a team. As the day draws closer, they meet both as department teams and the total store team, with every one of their colleagues. They hear directly from their store manager and members of the Nordstrom family, who attend every opening.

The final rally before the doors open is openly emotional as the team focuses on its collective achievement—getting the store ready for customers. The store manager offers words of inspiration and thanks for being part of the opening team. Each department within the store is recognized for its contributions. The rally is fun and upbeat—many of the departments bring signs and props, and they cheer, applaud, and sometimes do dances or skits when their department is mentioned.

When the doors are open for the first time, thousands of customers—who have been waiting outside for hours—stream into the store, sometimes shoulder-to-shoulder. There to greet them are the salespeople who are lined up along the entrance, handing out balloons and applauding the customers. The store is packed with vendor demonstrations, glasses of champagne, and lots of gifts. It's impossible to not to have fun.

We attended the opening of Nordstrom's store in Vancouver, British Columbia, which featured food trucks, photo booths, a live band, fun prizes, and a "Beauty Bash" outside the store, where customers got the latest scoop on beauty trends and received complimentary consultations, and free makeup applications by Nordstrom's makeup artists. The first 2,500 customers received a Nordstrom Beauty Bash tote.

Nordstrom partnered with the Canadian Breast Cancer Foundation on the event to raise awareness for the cause.

Have Fun and Give Back

When Nordstrom opens a full-line store in a new market, it's a big deal. The key is to come in "with all guns blazing," said Bruce. "I think we get off to a running start better than anybody. We say, 'Let's be beautiful, let's be great, let's have a beautiful opening party, let's have fun.' In a new market, we like to start off on the right foot, to give back something to the community before we open our doors. We donate lots of money to local charities and other good causes. We haven't made a cent yet, but we're going to do those things first."

To choose which beneficiaries it will partner with, Nordstrom's Charitable Giving team visits the community several months in advance to meet with nonprofits in the area. Once the recipients are selected, Nordstrom partners with them for a gala event, such as a formal celebration, a fashion show/benefit, or kids' tile-painting parties with hundreds of thousands of dollars going to those nonprofits.

"This is an opportunity for us to reach out to the community and learn what their greatest needs are and what we can do to support their efforts," said Terri Baldwin, director of Charitable Giving at Nordstrom. "It's also a time for us to share more about our approach to giving, our commitment to our communities, and our store opening plans."

Nordstrom doesn't do cookie cutter events. For example, when the company opened a store in Austin, Texas, the entertainment was a local band called Sour Bridges, which played "brown grass music" ("blue grass, but a little dirtier," according to the band's website) while 1,000 customers feasted on barbecue and other delicacies from local eateries.

Give Back

These kinds of efforts to give back epitomize what Nordstrom strives for—selfless service in all its forms to customers, coworkers, colleagues, suppliers, and the community. The company tries to be a good citizen and a good neighbor that is dedicated to finding ways to contribute to the common good.

Corporate social responsibility has become a benchmark for customer loyalty. A significant portion of today's consumers want to spend their money with companies that they believe are also good corporate citizens.

But don't forget that corporate social responsibility is a benchmark for employee loyalty as well. A good portion of the members of today's workforce want to work for a company that understand what it's like to be a good neighbor.

Although Nordstrom is in the business of selling stuff to consumers, the company wants its customers, employees, vendors, and shareholders to understand that it is also in the business of doing good while doing well. Nordstrom has had a long-running dialogue with its employees and customers to learn what matters most to them when it comes to being a good citizen, and it has created a comprehensive strategy of social responsibility based on the input of a task force of leaders from all areas of the company.

According to Nordstrom, the most frequently asked questions from both employees and customers concern the company's commitment to using recycled materials, supporting eco-friendly products, and offering responsible choices to its customers.

"When leaders create and insure alignment between the place where people feel connected and the actual day-to-day work that they do, reservoirs of energy and creativity are released," writes Dr. Jan Birchfield of Contemplative Leadership Development. We all have "a yearning for connection: The longing to be connected to the ongoing unfolding of life itself is inextricably linked to our longing to serve."

Nordstrom Cares

"We work hard to be a company our employees and our customers can be proud of," reads a Nordstrom statement. "For us, that means doing our best to support the many people and communities we serve. It also means respecting the environment by reducing our impact and conserving resources where we can. We strive to make people feel good and show that Nordstrom is a company that cares."

That statement can be found on a link on Nordstrom.com called "Nordstrom Cares," where the company details its progress and initiatives on all of its corporate responsibility initiatives.

Nordstrom lives by the phrase, "Leave It Better Than You Found It," which just happens to be the title of Bruce Nordstrom's memoir. The company holds itself accountable by setting goals and evaluating its progress toward meeting goals in recycling, transportation, paper and packaging, energy, water, human rights, natural and organic food offerings, and community support. Every year since 2009, Nordstrom makes available on its website, a lengthy and detailed progress report on Corporate Social Responsibility (CSR), "an opportunity to share our goals and hold ourselves accountable to them. We've used it to demonstrate progress and identify opportunities to improve."

When it comes to self-evaluation, Nordstrom is disarmingly honest. It will state whether its making progress or falling short of its goals. That honesty gives "Nordstrom Cares" credibility.

Nordstrom's CSR is built on two pillars: taking care of the communities where it does business and respecting the environment.

Here are examples of the Nordstrom Way of giving back to the community:

Cash Grants: Nordstrom donates 1 percent of all gift card sales to nonprofits in individual communities. The funds from this program support cash grants made by Nordstrom and its Employee Charitable Match program. This program is open to all employees who have been with the company for at least one year. It gives each employee $5,000 per fiscal year to match their personal donations to eligible nonprofits.

Each month on NordstromCares.com, the company spotlights some of the nonprofit organizations it supports through contributions and employee volunteers.

Treasure & Bond, Nordstrom's private label brand: Nordstrom donates 2.5 percent of net sales from T&B to organizations that empower youth. T&B products are in women's, girls', and men's apparel; women's shoes, handbags, and accessories; and girls' footwear.

Shoes That Fit, which is helping children in need in thousands of schools across the United States get new shoes and other necessities.

M★A★C VIVA GLAM: When customers purchase any MAC Viva Glam lipstick or lipgloss products, Nordstrom gives 100 percent of the proceeds to organizations that provide a wide range of services to people living with HIV/AIDS, including education, support, and funding for research.

Human rights: Although Nordstrom's stores are currently only in North America and Puerto Rico, Nordstrom is an international company in many ways. Nordstrom.com claims customers from more than 100 countries. And Nordstrom is also an international manufacturer of more than 50 brands of products, manufactured in more than 500 factories through its Nordstrom Product Group (NPG). NPG manufacturers have to adhere to Nordstrom's Partnership Guidelines for proper working conditions. Nordstrom hires a third party to audit all of the factories that make NPG merchandise.

To reflect the communities where it does business, Nordstrom has an aggressive Minority- and Women-Owned Supplier Diversity

Program, which it began in 1989, to attract qualified businesses to consider Nordstrom as a potential client. When Nordstrom enters a new market, the company cultivates minority-owned and women-owned vendors of office supplies, food, music, photography, and other services, including construction. This program helps form community contacts with a wide range of business and civic leaders, and it gives an opportunity to boost the economic vitality of the communities.

The second pillar of Nordstrom's corporate responsibility is being good stewards of the environment by developing inventive programs around recycling, packaging, sustainability, and other green concerns. Nordstrom is making concerted efforts on these fronts to reduce its carbon footprint. The company is looking at virtually every area in its far-flung operations: energy use and management, lighting technology, renewable and alternative energy sources. To make its delivery options more earth-friendly, Nordstrom is looking at ways to better optimize schedules, truck capacity, and gas efficiency.

The company is constantly looking at improving recycling and composting. When it comes to paper and packaging, when a customer places an order with Nordstrom for more than one item, it's Nordstrom's goal for the customer to receive all of those items in one box, if feasible. In Nordstrom's restaurants and specialty bars, the goal is to use as many sustainable products as possible.

Nordstrom solicits green or cost-saving suggestions from employees, and encourages them to share their ideas with whoever is in charge of that particular initiative. The men and women who come up with a good idea to create positive change are designated as "Nordstrom Cares Heroes."

The company has ongoing initiatives focusing on reducing greenhouse gas emissions, energy use, lighting technology, energy management, renewable and alternative energy sources, water use, transportation, conserving resources, recycling and composting, paper and packaging.

All gift boxes and shopping bags are made from 100 percent recycled content. "If it came from us, you can put it in the recycle bin," Nordstrom assures its customers.

Shopping bags from Nordstrom Rack are made of 80 percent recycled content, and they have an additive that helps them decompose in landfills in the event that they don't make it into a recycle bin.

All catalogs, annual reports, and paper-based employee communications are made with Forest Stewardship Council–certified stock with 30 percent postconsumer waste. Most Nordstrom gift cards are made of 50 percent preconsumer/post-industrial recycled PVC stock. All inks are soy-based.

In its stores and office buildings, Nordstrom labels all recycling containers and displays educational messaging in the hallways, meeting rooms, and near the cash wraps, and spreads the word through awareness fairs, manager meetings, and e-mails.

The restaurant division recycles all cups and napkins. All to-go bags and containers are recyclable. All brewed ice tea is organic, and all eggs are from cage-free hens. Organic matter is being composted in many stores.

Nordstrom wants to show its customers that fashion and the environment can coexist.

For example, Nordstrom took an abundant material—the plastic water bottle—and converted it into a stylish, versatile tote bag, made from 100-percent post-consumer-recycled material. Approximately ten 16-oz. water bottles went into the making of each bag. These bags were made from discarded material that otherwise would have been headed for landfills. The bag looked modern and felt strong. It stood up to rain, snow, sun, and sand, and could be washed and wiped clean. It also folded up into its own compact pouch, so it fit inside the customer's regular handbag. When fully expanded, the bag was big enough to hold two shoeboxes. Each tote featured an earth-friendly illustration by artist Ruben Toledo.

As it moves into its twelfth decade of business, Nordstrom's values have remained unchanged. Its strategy is built around a steadfast and constant belief that the customer remains the best filter for every business decision it makes, both large and small. An obsession with the customer experience continues to be what separates this company from the rest of the field.

Although the ways in which it takes care of customers must adapt with the times and the technology, the company's values remain constant and steadfast.

Bruce told us that his father, Everett, "had a unique ability to get to the heart of the matter. He believed strongly in the things that make our company unique and strong: Give the customer a good value, treat people fairly, allow everyone to contribute their thoughts and make their own mistakes, and finally, set a goal and devote yourself to its completion.

"The values of honesty and hard work, which he shared with his younger brothers, continue to this day to be the bedrock of our company," said Bruce. "We couldn't do what we've done if we didn't have those values, which manifest themselves in many different ways. Every day in every store in every region, hopefully, something positive is happening that will reinforce our reputation and make things better for our employees, our customers, and our communities."

And that is The Nordstrom Way.

About RSi

RSi is recognized worldwide as the premier authority on customer service. Cofounder Robert Spector is the author of several books on the subject, most notably the international bestsellers *The Nordstrom Way* and *Amazon: Get Big Fast*, as well as *The Mom & Pop Store: True Stories from the Heart of America*, in which Robert profiles small, entrepreneurial businesses, including his dad's butcher shop. He is an entertaining and inspiring thought leader who has worked with companies all over the world.

RSi's message and methodology, which was developed by cofounder breAnne O. Reeves, helps to guide companies of all kinds to create powerful, customer-focused cultures that deliver exemplary customer experiences and build lasting relationships. This methodology takes the form of The Relationship Model™ (TRM), which is based on the belief that in business, as in life, love wins. What happens when we love? We gain respect and loyalty—for employees, customers, and the other stakeholders who contribute to a brand's success.

We believe that making a series of small but significant changes can elevate your organization to become the Nordstrom of your industry.

While we cut our teeth with Fortune 500 companies, we love, understand, respect, and appreciate small, entrepreneurial businesses, which is how we integrate mom-and-pop thinking into corporate organizations. Here are our offerings:

Keynote Programs

Robert's dynamic and engaging keynote program explains (in story form) the core values and principles of the world-class customer service cultures he has written about. This program sets the stage for creating, encouraging, and sustaining a superior customer service experience.

We customize our program(s) according to the needs and goals of your organization, and support your customer service initiatives.

Consulting and Advisory

Designed and facilitated by breAnne O. Reeves and her team, our customized consulting and advisory support help to create a collaborative environment that extracts hidden wisdom, while generating fresh approaches to the employee and customer experience. We help you identify existing and new opportunities, and co-create strategies for efficient implementation. The ideas that are generated during our collaboration are translated into reports and tangible strategies for your organization.

Do you want to become the Nordstrom of your industry? Please contact us: info@robertspector.com.

Index

Page references followed by *fig* indicate an illustrated figure.